Finding the Edge

Finding the Edge

MY LIFE ON THE ICE

KAREN CHEN

WITH NATALIE ENGLAND

HARPER

An Imprint of HarperCollinsPublishers

Glossary of figure skating terms on pages 179–202 courtesy of
US Figure Skating and the International Skating Union
Silhouettes by denniro and mr.Timmi / Shutterstock Images
Photos courtesy of the author

ISBN 978-0-06-282268-0

17 18 19 20 21   PC/LSCC   10 9 8 7 6 5 4 3 2 1
❖
First Edition

To my family and friends,
whose love and support is truly indescribable

Contents

FOREWORD

IT WAS SEVERAL YEARS AGO WHEN I FIRST HEARD
about a promising young skater from my hometown in
California. Karen Chen had just won the Intermediate
Ladies title at the US Figure Skating Championships, and
there was a lot of talk about how good she was. People
kept asking if I'd seen her yet, so naturally I was curious
and wanted to watch her skate. As an Asian American
skater from Fremont myself, I felt a connection with
Karen before even meeting her.

We had our first meeting at the Fremont ice rink
when I sat in on one of Karen's lessons. She was only
eleven at the time, and I wasn't sure if she even knew

who I was. But, boy, was I thrilled to meet her—and boy, was I dazzled from the very beginning. I remember watching Karen work on her double axel; she was pushing to get more speed and flow while skating into the jump and through the landing. She executed some beautiful double axels, and I was impressed that she had such incredible power for such a petite girl, not to mention the speed and height of her jumps. Yes, she had a few bobbles, too, but she took in all of her coach's instructions and tried to apply them for next time. Some attempts were better and some were not, but no matter what, Karen exuded a determination to improve. Everything about Karen made me smile. There are many gifted skaters in this sport, but you don't always *feel* something from them. You don't always understand their way of doing things the way I did with Karen.

As I left the rink and thought about this tiny young skater, I couldn't help but make comparisons. I saw a great deal of my young self in Karen: her shyness, her ability to take instruction and apply it, her determination to get better, her desire and willingness to work hard, and of course her competitiveness. I was a fan of Karen's from that day on. She had a special something that I could feel—a spark that shone when she skated.

Karen has grown as a skater and young lady over the last few years, and there have already been many highlights to her promising career. She holds a US Championship title at the Novice Ladies level (and it was a special one in front of a local crowd at the 2012 San Jose US Championships!). She skated at a high competitive level in the junior category before debuting at the senior level in 2015 with a giant splash and an incredible third-place finish. This impressive debut turned the eyes of the figure-skating world on her. Two years later, Karen stormed into the 2017 US Championships with confidence and determination. She skated nearly flawless routines in both her short and long programs, thereby becoming the newly crowned US Ladies champion!

It all sounds so magical, right?

Well, with the highs come the lows. We all have challenges in life, and Karen is no exception. She makes the ongoing grueling commute back and forth from Northern California, where her family is based, to Southern California, where her current coach is. She is also being homeschooled while her training regimen ramps up for the 2018 Olympic year. And even during the early stages of her competitive career, there were hurdles. When Karen was competing as a junior skater, she suffered a terrible injury. But did breaking her ankle keep her down? No. She came back the following year as a senior competitor, and that's when she earned the bronze medal. A struggle with skating boot issues also kept Karen out of contention for the US Championships in 2016. But she persevered and got herself back on track for the following season. And that determination was rewarded a hundred times over when she became the United States Ladies champion in 2017. Karen has pushed through and overcome many obstacles, and she has made many sacrifices to achieve her accomplishments.

Looking at what Karen has endured and how she continues to pursue her dream, I feel such admiration and pride. Although she is still chasing her ultimate dream of representing her country at the Olympic Games, she is already an exemplary athlete and a young woman with a strong work ethic, dedication, tenacity, and yes, some of that kick-butt attitude any fierce competitor needs.

Karen Chen will be a name in the books of figure-skating history, for sure—and in the meantime, she is an inspiring role model for anyone chasing a dream. I hope my own two daughters read this book and learn what it's like to be passionate about something and what it takes—both the victories *and* the defeats—to have success. Thank you, Karen, for sharing your story with us.

KRISTI YAMAGUCHI
Olympic champion, two-time World champion, and US champion

PROLOGUE

US Figure Skating Championships
Thursday, January 19, 2017
Kansas City, Missouri
Short Program

I DON'T WANT TO BE AFRAID. I WANT TO BE A BIRD.

A bird doesn't think about falling; a bird doesn't know what it means to cry. Birds simply lift their wings and glide, like the whole world is theirs. I want to be that kind of bird. I want to fly.

Ice skating is the closest I get to flying—it's the only time I feel weightless and free. Skating is the most natural thing in the world, my blades carrying me as they cut edges into the ice, as I push and pull myself around the rink and then up through the air. The ice is my second home. On the ice, I am neither shy nor soft-spoken; it's the place where I feel completely comfortable. That's how I want to skate in my short program tonight: comfortable, joyful, happy. And when I'm out there alone under the spotlight, I want everyone watching me to feel those same emotions.

My coach tells me I'm fierce. She says there's fearlessness in my eyes, and toughness, too, when I'm focusing on what I want. For me, life has been this scary roller coaster: sometimes I'm at the bottom, not sure what I'm truly looking for, and sometimes I'm at the top, eyes locked on my goal. After all these years, pushing and pushing and pushing—*one more, Karen, just do one more*—it's finally time to let go. The negative momentum that drives you to the bottom of the roller coaster can start to work for you, if you let it. Hit the bottom and rise. A champion doesn't worry about what others say or all the things that might go wrong. A champion is calm, ready, steady.

The song I'm skating to tonight, "On Golden Pond," is delicate and light, reminding me of the bird I want to be. I can understand this music. I can *feel* it. And I'll bring that emotion with me onto the ice. I'll use my body and my movements like instruments to express emotions I can't put into words.

Before the first piano notes begin, the birds—I think they're loons—start calling to one another. *What are they saying? What do they want us to know?* It could be daybreak, a new beginning, hope. Whatever you're looking for, now is the time to find it. Now is the time for *me* to find what I've been looking for since I was five years old, since I put on my first pair of skating boots and tried to fly.

The loons' calls give way to piano chords, and my moment has arrived.

I am here in Kansas City, under these lights, in front of my family, surrounded by hundreds of people, in the center of this rink. I am competing at the US Figure Skating Championships.

I don't want to be afraid.

I want to be a bird.

I want to be a national champion.

CHAPTER 1

COMING TO LIFE

WHEN I CLOSE MY EYES, I SEE TAIWAN. I SEE GREEN, the welcoming expanse of lush mountains, big and blanketed with trees. Sometimes I even try to remember the smell, the savory scents of streams and fishing nets, the sugary perfume of fruit ripening in the garden.

I may be a California girl at heart—it's where I was born, where I live, where I imagine I'll always want to be—but California isn't what I see when my mind drifts to the warm, wonderful memories of my childhood. Instead, I see the rivers where I fished with my grandfather, the rink in Taipei where my grandmother took me to skate, the garden at my grandparents' house bursting with papaya and turnips. I wonder if other people do this, think about their past and the different moments they've captured in their minds, then think to themselves, *That's so sweet. I always want to remember this. I love this memory.* I do that all the time. And in my memory, the moments are always green. They're always Taiwan.

My mom's name is Hsiu-Hui (pronounced Showei) and my dad's name is, well, he goes by Ken. My dad also has a Chinese name, but to be honest, I'm not sure how to pronounce it properly. These days, I do try to speak Chinese as often as I can, especially with my parents, but it basically comes out as a mix of Chinese and English. My Chinese used to be much better, when I was spending more time outside the United States.

Beginning when I was around two years old, I'd go visit my mom's parents in Taiwan for two months, then come home to California for two months. My grandmother always flew with me to and from Taiwan, and the flight attendants would marvel to her that I was quiet and easy to handle. "She's not fussy at all," they'd say. I was so small, even the stiff airline seats felt cushy and comfortable.

Taiwan is an island, and Grandma and Grandpa live near the capital city of Taipei on the northernmost tip. Snuggled in a basin, surrounded by mountain ranges,

Taipei's beautiful greenery almost camouflages what a big, bustling city it is. My grandparents, who are rice farmers, live there among millions of others, and their house is on a decently sized plot of land that's been passed down in my family for many generations. Any which way you look, there's greenery and vegetation. Plants everywhere! Grandma has a garden, which was one of my most cherished places to spend time as a kid. She always cooked my favorite dishes using whatever she was growing. Grandma makes magic with vegetables. I'd devour heaps of sautéed spinach, scooping it up with rice and noodles. Because of her, I've always loved eating colorful food picked fresh from the ground. She would take me into the garden with her, and I'd get to help choose fruits and vegetables. She showed me which ones were ripe and which ones needed to grow a little longer. Sometimes she'd leave the low-hanging fruit for me to pick and toss into our barrel when we walked by on our way back to the house. Fruit tastes better in Taiwan— or at least it tasted better out of my grandma's garden. Bananas, papayas, dragon fruit: I ate everything and as much of it as I could.

As for my grandpa, he loves to fish the way my grandma loves to garden. He'd take me fishing all the time, and it quickly became one of my favorite things to do. Reservoirs and lakes and rivers are easy to come by where my grandparents live, and my grandfather always knew just where to go. I never had any clue where we were heading, but that didn't matter. I was with Grandpa, and that meant I was safe.

There was this one place near the mountains, where the waters were calm and shallow, and Grandpa would let me wander out there by myself. I'd splash around, fascinated by this whole different world living in crystal-blue water so clear I could see the shrimp darting back and forth.

Other slick creatures zipped around just below the surface, a little bigger than bugs but not big enough to be fish. "Grandpa, what are these adorable things?" I asked.

"Tadpoles."

I even thought the frogs were cute.

Once I was old enough to be in school, my visits to Taiwan became less frequent. But these days, my family tries to make the trip at least once a year so we can all gather together—Grandpa, Grandma, aunts, uncles, cousins. The next time I go back, I hope Grandpa takes me fishing.

My brother, Jeffrey, was born in California when I was only three, so I don't remember much about my life before he was in it. I am very shy, whereas Jeffrey is very outgoing. When we had friends or guests over to the house, he was the star, always goofing off and making people laugh, zooming around the house in his little toy car. I stuck close to my parents, hiding behind their legs and only coming out of my shell once I warmed up to the visitors.

Despite the differences in our personalities, Jeffrey and I were sidekicks from the very beginning. My parents both like being active outdoors, doing things like Rollerblading and hiking, and Jeffrey and I are no different. Whenever we had free time, and our parents weren't busy being hardworking software engineers, we'd go to these big fields near our house in Fremont, California, and run around and play catch.

I'm grateful that my parents were open-minded and didn't force me down a certain path early on, instead exposing me to all kinds of activities. They let me try different hobbies, and I was able to figure out what I loved doing. I took some ballet classes and some Chinese dance classes. Mostly, though, I danced at home. My mom still has videos of me dressed up and dancing to the soundtrack of the movie *Mulan*. In the videos, Jeffrey is bobbing and playing around me, my tiny little twin dressed, for whatever reason, in a bumblebee costume.

Then one day when I was five, my parents proposed a new idea, an opportunity to try something scary and exciting:

"Let's go ice skating," they said.

CHAPTER 2

FINDING A FRIEND

I WISH I COULD REMEMBER THE FIRST TIME I LACED
up a pair of skating boots and slid out onto that big, frozen circle. After all, who wouldn't want to remember the moment they fell in love? In the sea of my colorful and vivid childhood memories, that one simply isn't there. Oftentimes you don't realize just how important something will be in the moment that it happens.

As a beginning skater, luckily I wasn't what my first teacher, Crystal Araujo, called a spaghetti skater. You know, when your arms and legs go limp as soon as your blades touch the ice? There were about ten little first-time skaters in my group lesson at the rink in Dublin,

California, half an hour's drive from our house. Some of them were spaghetti skaters, but not me. I could stand and I had good balance, probably thanks to my dad, who always encouraged me to run and tumble outside. He gave me the gift of athleticism.

Crystal says she was able to work with me and teach me skills on my very first day. Even though I don't remember that, what I do remember is how the ice made me feel and, more specifically, how it made me cry. I was very, very shy—extremely shy, the absolute most shy. I barely talked. That first day, I didn't want to confront people. I didn't want to talk to anyone. I certainly didn't want to skate in front of strangers.

I think the shyness had to do with not wanting to embarrass myself. I had this nagging little voice in my head: *Oh, Karen, you're going to look like a fool.*

And at the time, I didn't realize I could tell that voice to be quiet. I didn't understand the power of mind over body. I didn't realize that, by making a scene and crying, I was embarrassing myself even more. I was only five, after all.

As soon as I got on the ice, though, I was completely fine. It was the before part that had freaked me out. Within an hour I went from a shy, fearful little girl clinging to her mom's hands, reluctant to leave the boards and join her classmates, to this free and joyful skater.

Yes, I was only traveling in consecutive circles around an enclosed ice rink, but to me, it felt like I was going places, like I was discovering something new and someone new. I was discovering a girl who wasn't afraid.

By the end of my first session, my mom had made her decision: that was my first and last group class. As soon as Crystal skated me off the ice, my mom said, "When can we start private lessons?" And that was the beginning of my training.

Perhaps surprisingly, it was never falling that scared me. (It must have helped that I was only about a foot off the ground, so if I did fall, I didn't have very far to go!) As I quickly learned, falling is a reality of skating. It's going to happen, so you just have to get back up time after time. Plus, Crystal encouraged her skaters to buy volleyball knee pads to cushion our landings. I had knee pads, hip pads, and elbow pads. I didn't wear a helmet, but I was very protected everywhere else. And each time I did fall, I thought it was hilarious. Little kids are strange. . . .

Not to mention that my mom was always there, right beside the ice and right behind the boards, and her presence gave me a lot of confidence. I felt safe enough to try new things and push outside my comfort zone. It can be intimidating when you start to progress through glides and you begin to spin! Having my mom there made me less afraid to pick up my foot and get myself off the ice and into the air. And if I did fall, or miss a rotation, or shy away from a new, more complicated technique, I could always hear my mom calling out to me: "Try it again. You can do better. Do it again."

Although I initially learned to skate in California, there also happened to be an ice-skating rink near my grandparents' house in Taiwan. That first day we tried it out, the whole endeavor felt odd. My grandparents drove me into the city, and we parked in a multilevel parking garage and took an elevator up to the rink. Even though I wasn't taking classes or skating in a group, I still didn't feel comfortable being in a new place with new people. Just like that first day at my home rink a few months before, I had this fear that I would stand out for the wrong reasons. I was still scared to embarrass myself.

My grandparents could sense my reluctance to step out on the ice (maybe because I was shielding myself beside the boards . . .). They told me that it was perfectly fine if I wanted to leave, that I didn't have to skate. But I did want to skate! I wanted to be on the ice! It was such a dilemma, like having an argument with myself. My little internal voice told me to walk away because I would inevitably do something dumb and people would notice.

Then I heard something else. I heard my mom's voice

in my head. *You got this. Keep going.*

So I did.

Finally, I took that the first step—which, in my mind, felt more like a giant leap—and went onto the ice. And once I started skating and feeling those rushing sensations, everything was right.

After that, my grandparents ended up taking me to the rink almost every day. I'd skate out onto the ice by myself and feel the hug of freedom. There's an independence that comes with getting on your boots and pushing out onto your blades. And hour after hour, skating alone with my grandparents nearby, my love for the ice deepened with every cut of the blade.

The coldness of the rink disappeared as soon as I started moving on the ice. The body heats up, partially from the anticipation of going out on that edge to the very tip of control and partially from every muscle in your body firing to work in coordination. The cold air tingling my warm cheeks gave me such a rush, and the ripping chords of my edges slicing through the ice were my own personal soundtrack every time I skated.

On the ice, it's the blade that helps me as I skate. It's my closest, most reliable friend. Everything comes down to this quarter-inch piece of steel with two edges, an outside edge and an inside edge. Speed, balance, and control all come from strong edges, the deep, crisp figures that the blades carve into the ice. Practicing and improving edge quality is a lifelong endeavor. The edge compresses and cuts, creating the friction that propels the skater up and back, down and across, over and over and over again. The edge connects the skater to the ice, which is why the blade and the edge are everything.

Maybe I don't remember my first California skating lesson because it was at that rink in Taiwan where I actually fell in love with skating.

Circle after circle, I developed my technique by doing my own thing—no teacher, no coach, no Mom. I gained command of stroking skills, those necessary steps that connect the elements of a routine. I learned swift and controlled methods for entering and exiting jumps and spins. No matter who you are as a skater—whether you're known for stomach-dropping, gravity-defying jumps or head-turning spins—we all draw on the same set of fundamental techniques. There's even a best way to fall. (Falls are unpredictable, but falling on your butt is considered ideal; I always tried to slide with my fall, and it was probably the slippery sensation on my bottom that tickled me to fits of laughter.) In Taiwan, I began to hone the skills that would carry me through the rest of my skating career. I began to see that skating was something

I was actually good at. In that city skating rink, surrounded by mountain slopes of towering, lush green trees, I discovered the thing I loved more than anything in the entire world.

CHAPTER 3

FIGURING IT OUT

AFTER I DECIDED TO PURSUE SKATING MORE
intensely, Crystal went from being my first teacher to
my first coach. She herself was an accomplished and
talented skater, and she trained her skaters to compete
because that was how she'd been taught. She was one of
the only coaches at that rink in Dublin who encouraged
us to prepare *off* the ice in order to make ourselves better
on the ice.

On practice days before we'd start skating, we went
through a series of warm-up stretches so our bodies were
limber and ready to get the most out of the session. She
also encouraged us to work on our movements at home.

Even if you aren't at the rink, you can work on certain techniques to improve your form, especially when you're first learning how to jump. Movements like bending into and jumping from your knees, rotating through the air, and gaining height—these can all be drilled on dry land (minus the skates, of course). Early on, my mom convinced me how important stretching and warming up were because, by nature, I tend to tighten up stiff as a board. I'd spend my evenings stretching in front of the TV, learning to embrace stretching pain as good pain.

I was a fast learner, but I also worked hard. I wanted to do everything right the very first time. Often that wouldn't happen, since skating is both awkward and frustrating—it takes a while to get the feeling and the timing down. I didn't mind putting in the necessary hours on the ice, even after our lessons ended. I was happy to skate as long as I had to until I got a move right. Crystal and I found a rhythm that worked for us: she would teach me something, I'd learn how to practice on my own or at home, and then when I got back on the ice, I would see improvement. Once I had one technique nailed, Crystal added another, and I repeated the process. As a result of all these repetitions, my moves advanced pretty quickly and I started to see consistent improvement.

Because I was so little, I often attracted attention at the ice rink. "Wow," a parent once remarked to Crystal, "your skates are as big as her legs!" And it was true: I was tiny, yet I was doing what the big girls were doing.

The first time I performed my program was at a small showcase event at my home rink in Dublin. There weren't any judges or scores; it was an opportunity to get out under the lights and feel the rush of being on center ice. I skated to *Sleeping Beauty*, and Crystal choreographed the whole thing. She'd given me a lot of markers, and because ice rinks are designed for hockey players, we used those colored lines and circles to help guide my routine. I'd start on one line, following it while doing my various moves, and then go to another line. That's how we connected the different parts of my program.

I was only six years old when I entered my first competition. I'd learned to skate, I'd learned a few techniques, and now it was time to see how I could do against other girls. For the competition—which had real live judges and trophies for the winners—we traveled across the bay and into San Francisco. And I would be competing against older girls! The only things that felt normal were the ice and my soft pink velvet dress. Everything else was new and overwhelming. When all the skaters were sent out on the ice for a warm-up, I was confused. *What am I supposed to do? Should I be practicing my whole routine, or just skating around the rink?* Of course I didn't dare ask anyone, even my parents or my coach. I didn't want to let on that I was completely clueless. I looked around and figured something out. *Do a few single jumps and a spin,* I urged myself. And that's what I did.

At least I knew that when my turn came, I was supposed to skate to my pose and start my *Sleeping Beauty* program. I had practiced over and over, and I knew it by heart. I was still pretty young, and I didn't have a lot of moves, but of the ones I did have, we'd incorporated every single one into my routine.

Right before on I went on the ice, Crystal reminded me to listen to the music: "If you end early, add some extra hand movements. Improvise so you're in sync with the length of the song."

I nodded. And the funny thing was, I really wasn't that nervous.

When my turn came, I skated out there, took my pose, did my program, bowed, and got off the ice. My parents were in shock. So was I. I hadn't skated like a shy little girl. I'd had a few hiccups during the performance, yet those mistakes hadn't shaken me. I almost fell and then managed to turn a spiral into a wobbly glide. I felt like I'd been in a zone, even able to add a few extra moves at the end to match the length of the routine with the length of the song.

For those two minutes on the ice, I really believed I was the princess from *Sleeping Beauty*. And I was rewarded for my performance by being awarded my very first trophy.

Not long after that competition, Crystal delivered some difficult news: she could no longer be my coach. She had a little daughter of her own on the way—which was wonderful, and I was happy for her. But I was also sad. A good coach is hard to find. A good coach is someone who takes the time to listen to and understand a skater. With me, Crystal knew I was shy, and when people came up and asked me questions, she often answered for me. She was protective, which I appreciated. As much as I loved skating and practicing, sometimes I had bad days when I wasn't energetic and didn't want to be on the ice. Even then, Crystal managed to focus my attention, letting me color or draw first in order to get me in the mood. I barely talked to my kindergarten teacher; it was Crystal who'd helped me find my voice as a kid.

Crystal wanted to make sure I was set up to continue on my path, so she told me and my parents about coaches who were willing to take me on. One of them was Crystal's mentor coach, the person who'd trained her to be a competitor and who'd taught her the off-ice routines that had, in turn, helped *me* grow and develop.

So, when I was six, I started skating in Fremont, California, with a personal coach named Sherri Krahne-Thomas. Her mentor coach, Gilley Nicholson (who'd also coached Crystal), soon joined in to take me to the next level.

CHAPTER 4

PRACTICING PERFECT

YOU KNOW HOW SANTA CLAUS IS DESCRIBED—ICY white hair and cuddly body? Well, that was my coach Gilley to a T. He was the quintessential grandfather-type: supportive and encouraging, creating an environment where it felt safe to go out on the edge and try something new and daring.

Although fundamental skills like figures and footwork are an important foundation for every skater, no one can deny that the jumps are the moves that get all the attention. Jumps are what everyone watches for. And that includes the judges, who grade us on difficulty and precision in execution.

With jumping, the jump itself isn't the scary part. It's having to *land* the jump that makes you nervous. Gilley was the one who helped me overcome those fears as I went from single-rotation jumps to the doubles and triples that are required in your program as you progress from one competition level to the next.

"No, I don't think I can do that," I'd say when Gilley instructed me to attempt a new, scarier move.

Because Gilley believed in me, he'd reply, "Yes, you can do it. I know you can do it."

So I'd try it a few times.

"That's a great try," he'd say.

I'd try it a few more times.

"Those were great tries," he'd say again.

And then I'd actually land it. Trust me, it wasn't clean or even close to perfect, but I'd land it.

Gilley was always telling me to trust myself, and he created an atmosphere that made it easy to. I credit both Gilley and Sherri with teaching me my basics and also bringing my personality as a skater to life.

Now, that's Gilley. As for Sherri, she was the disciplinarian and the much stricter one. If it hadn't been for Sherri teaching me all the best positions for spins and flexibility, I wouldn't be where I am today. Sherri had no choice but to be rules-oriented: even though I happened to be a very quiet kid, most of the young skaters she was training talked up a storm during practice. She had learned that to be effective, you had to be strict and make the student focus. It was the only way to get results.

The best thing a skater can do is listen. Gilley and Sherri were my coaches, and when they told me to do something, I'd nod my head and do it. I didn't have second thoughts. I didn't have opinions. My mind-set was "This is what I need to do, and I'm going to go do it." A good coach understands the individual skater and offers guidance and direction accordingly. But even if a coach is the best in the world, results still depend on the skater's attitude and how hard she's willing to work.

At the beginning, as I was exploring the world of skating and gradually finding my competitive passion, I was only going to the rink on the weekends. On Saturdays, I was willing to get up very early to go skate. It's amazing what's possible when you're young and full of energy! I also didn't have much of a choice: in order to get the necessary ice time with Gilley and Sherri at Sharks Ice in Fremont, I had to be there first thing in the morning. That's just when the ice was available to little skaters like me. Luckily, the rink was only a short drive from our house.

Then, in second grade, I began practicing during the week both before and after school. Skating competitions consist of two events: the short program and the long program (also known as the free skate). The short is always performed first, has a required number of technical elements, and is, as you might have guessed, shorter than the long program. Skaters can pick and choose the elements that best showcase their skills when developing their long program, hence the name free skate. At practice, I'd usually skate pieces of my short or long program in the morning, and then in the afternoon sessions, we'd work specifically on technical elements like jumps and spins. It wasn't just me and my coaches out on the ice during these practices; there were many other skaters working on their skills, and you learned quickly to be respectful of everyone's space and what they were working on.

For my morning sessions, I practiced from seven to eight thirty. Each night I went to bed excited, knowing that in the morning, I'd be getting up and doing something I loved. I'd wake up between four and five o'clock, eat a bowl of oatmeal to put something warm in my belly before getting out on the cold ice, and then head to the rink. And then after school, I'd go straight to the rink from class, and Jeffrey, who was such a good sport, would always come with me. I'm sure he got bored from playing hours of video games while I skated. Sometimes he'd even resort to flying paper airplanes in the lobby.

Once I hit middle school, I started off every weekday in the principal's office. If you were late—and I was always late because of practice—you had to go to the office and get a tardy slip. My desk had a whole drawer full of tardy slips. My fifth-grade homeroom teacher, Mrs. Mead, was strict and demanded our best behavior, but she knew I had skating practice early every morning and was very understanding of my situation.

Eventually it got to the point where I didn't even need to hand Mrs. Mead a tardy slip anymore. I'd open the door to the classroom, take one step inside, and the whole class would turn toward me: "Good morning, Karen."

"Hi," I'd reply.

I have to give a lot of credit to Mrs. Mead, who taught me how to focus and how to be responsible and organized, which helped me become a better all-around student as well as a better skater. As I've mentioned, I take pride in doing things the right way, and in Mrs. Mead's class, doing things the right way meant keeping a detailed planner with due dates and upcoming assignments. It helped me stay on top of all my different responsibilities in school, on the rink, and at home.

What about homework? you might be wondering. *When did you fit that in?* Well, I did homework in the car, I did homework at recess, I even brought my homework to lunch. Sometimes my friends joined in and we'd do it together, which meant we'd finish faster. I knew I had to save time in my day wherever possible so that I could go to sleep on the early side and not feel cranky when I woke up at dawn the next morning. For instance, on the days I decided to wear yoga pants to school—because I hated jeans—I changed back into my skating skirt while riding in the car to the rink. I even figured out how to do it while wearing a seat belt! I hated to be lazy. I even hated the word *lazy*. I always worked hard and gave everything 100 percent. Whether it was a homework assignment or a spin or a whole routine, I'd do things over and over and over and over again until they were right. That's repetition; that's how you improve. You don't get better by practicing what's wrong. You have to continually pour your energy into getting it right—until the moment you do.

Regardless of whether it was weekday or weekend practice, my mom was always at the rink watching me, and when she knew I could do better, she'd encourage me: "Do it again. You got this," just like she had when I was training with Crystal. You might be getting the sense that I'm kind of a perfectionist, and you're right. I think my mom is a perfectionist, too.

I am exceptionally fortunate because my mom was

allowed to work from home, which meant she could drive me to the rink and from the rink and to school and to home. And at night after I was done training, tucked away in bed, dreaming about the next morning's steaming bowl of oatmeal and triple lutzes, my mom had to work. Sometimes she'd work until past midnight, sleep a few hours, then get up to take me to workouts. It was very, very hard on her.

Besides being my constant supporter next to the ice, my mom was also the most incredible seamstress. At first we were ordering my competition dresses online, but they were itchy and irritated my skin. My mom figured out which parts were itchy, and then she figured out how to make them not itchy. From there, she gradually learned how to make my dresses. For my pre-juvenile, juvenile, intermediate, novice, and first year junior, she made all those dresses. She loved making dresses for me, and I loved taking her support and energy with me on the ice when I performed.

Sometimes my mom would stay up all night tending to the beading.

"Mommy, it's fine," I'd say.

"No, it's missing something. I want to add more stones."

See, I told you: perfectionist.

These days a special designer creates each of my performance dresses, but sometimes my mom still insists on sewing my exhibition pieces. Now my older dresses are all packed away in a closet—special mementos with special memories that will never be forgotten.

CHAPTER 5

PUSHING THROUGH

FROM THAT POINT ON, SKATING PRETTY MUCH consumed my family's entire life—even Jeffrey eventually gave in to his figure-skating destiny: around 2012 when he was ten, he put away his video games and began to train as a skater. If Jeffrey and I weren't at school, we were either at the rink or driving to or from the rink. And in the car, Jeffrey and I watched skating DVDs. We had recordings of the 1998 Nagano Olympics and some World Championships, and we watched them over and over. Jeffrey was obsessed with Evgeni Plushenko, the Russian skater who was a four-time Olympic medalist, three-time World champion, seven-time European champion, four-time Grand Prix Final champion, and ten-time Russian national champion. Our whole family would sit on the couch and watch Evgeni's performances after eating dinner and before going to bed.

I fiercely admired Michelle Kwan, two-time Olympic medalist, five-time World champion, and nine-time US champion. I think it was my dad who found the book she wrote, *Heart of a Champion*, and gave it to me. In it, she talks about how when the Zamboni would come out to clean the ice, she would tell the driver, "Just give me one more minute. I still want to do this move, and this jump, and this routine," and it's stuck with me ever since. Before I can leave the ice, I feel like I should do one more of this, one more of that. Afterward, I'm finally satisfied with myself and with my effort, and I'm ready to pack up, go home, and prepare to start again the next day.

Through my twice-daily practices, I continued to develop and add to my skills, and the US Figure Skating Tests were key indicators for my development. These tests set the national standard for skills. Your highest test passed determines the level you enter in a competition. It's kind of like karate, where an athlete progresses through the different belts, ultimately aiming to achieve a black belt. In skating, what you want to achieve is the senior level. On your way to senior, there are seven levels: pre-preliminary, preliminary, pre-juvenile, juvenile, intermediate, novice, junior, and then senior. Each level increases in difficulty, and builds on the techniques from the earlier ones. The skating club I joined in Fremont—the Peninsula Skating Club—organized tests at our rink, Sharks Ice, and on the testing days, three US Figure Skating Association (USFSA) judges would visit and grade our test patterns.

There are two testing tracks sanctioned by the USFSA, each with the eight levels within it. The first testing track is called Moves in the Field, and it's a baseline test to make sure a skater has all her fundamental skills, like posture, strength, power, edge quality, and quickness. The tests consist of four to six patterns that must be completed clockwise and counterclockwise, on both feet, and on both the inside and outside edges. I did this first test when I was six, and three years later when I was nine, I passed my senior-level moves in the field test. Once I had passed all those basic skills tests, I moved on to the second testing track: the free skate progression. The free skate tests move through the same eight levels, but test harder elements like jumps and spins—components that are performed in competitive programs. The level of free skate test a skater has passed determines a competition category.

Because progression has to do with mastery of all skating elements, age isn't necessarily a factor. However,

I did stand out for passing my senior-level fundamental tests at the age of nine. And then, as I began entering (and winning!) more and more local and regional preliminary and pre-juvenile competitions, I attracted plenty of attention. Unlike when I was skating with Crystal and people good-naturedly commented about her feet being longer than my legs, not everything being said about me at this point in my life was sweet. Sherri stopped my mom and me in the parking lot one night after practice. "Your child is exceptional," Sherri said, looking straight into my mom's eyes. "I think she's going to go far. You're going to deal with a lot of stuff. Parents will talk about her because she stands out, and not everyone is nice. They don't say nice things always."

Multiple doctors and physical therapists have told me that I have an extremely high pain tolerance, which is both good and bad. It's good because I can tolerate discomfort and push through. It's bad because sometimes I don't listen to my body when it's telling me I need to stop pushing. Instead, I talk over it: *Oh, this is perfectly okay. It's normal. Keep going. Don't be lazy.* I believe most competitive athletes have the ability to overcome some pain. For me, it's hard to find the perfect equation between overcoming my pain and respecting that pain means something is wrong. That particular balance has always been a bit of a struggle for me.

When I was nine, I broke my right ankle for the first time. The day I broke it, I was in a Saturday training session, running through one of my programs. By the final few minutes, I was exhausted. But I wanted to do my program one more time. *Push through,* I told myself. *You're not lazy.*

I had this combination—a jump into a spin—called a death drop. The death drop is a flying spin, and you need a deep edge to push powerfully into the takeoff. Your arms help lift you off the ice, and then both legs are split, parallel to the ice. The landing requires you to dig the tip of your toe pick in hard, burying it into the ice, and then you end up in a sit spin.

When I landed, something cracked. I couldn't hold my toe for the proper landing, and I slammed into the ice, my right ankle catching the fall. It was really painful. It was pain I couldn't forget about, talk away, or push through. This time, something was definitely wrong.

We went to the emergency room for X-rays and found out that a tiny piece of bone had chipped out of my ankle. That little piece was now floating around in my ankle somewhere. The only way to reattach the bone was surgery, but reattaching it wasn't actually necessary, so we just left it to float. (To this day you can still feel a bump where the tissue has grown all around it.) Even though I didn't need surgery, I did have to take time off to heal. It was the first period of my life I wasn't allowed to skate, and I was very sad. Physically and emotionally, I wanted to be on the ice.

But I knew I had to rest. The best shot I had of getting back into the rink as soon as possible was listening to my body (for once) and taking it easy. I took my rehab so seriously that when my family traveled to Taiwan during my winter break from school, I didn't even walk around. When my family went fishing and hiking, my dad carried me.

One of my grandmothers had gifted me a jade necklace when I was born, but my mother had never given it to me and I had never worn it. In Taiwanese culture, jade necklaces are supposed to bring luck, and they are handed down from generation to generation. "When I was a little girl," my mother explained, "my mom gave me a jade necklace. I felt safe wearing it."

After I broke my ankle, my mother remembered that I had a jade necklace. She found it, gave it to me, and told me to wear it and never take it off.

CHAPTER 6

MAKING SACRIFICES

GILLEY USED TO ASK ALL HIS STUDENTS, "WHAT IS your goal?"

Their answer was often the same: "I want to go to the Olympics."

Even in his grandfatherly way, Gilley didn't beat around the bush: "Then you better buy your tickets now. They're pretty hard to get."

And that's the harsh, true reality of the whole thing. Everyone wants to make it to the Olympics, to the top of the podium. Actually getting there is another thing entirely.

But if you were prepared to sacrifice, to give everything

you had in order to make it to the Olympics, Gilley said there was no secret formula other than work, work, work. "It's really simple," he told me once. "If you're playing the piano, you have to know the keys. Stretch your fingers out and hit the keys. To do it, you rehearse it over and over. Skating is the same. It's rehearsal. Over and over. Tick, tick, tick."

From Gilley I learned that champions make a habit of doing what most people find boring or uncomfortable. Seemingly simple acts, like packing my bag for the rink each day, were specialized to a science. Just like my fifth-grade planner, I kept almost everything in my life neat and organized. (My bedroom was another story, and my mom thankfully let it go. She says you have to express yourself somehow!) My skating bag was always stuffed with extra layers of clothing like vests and scarves, as well as quick and easy snacks, like fresh fruit (my favorite). Back then, I used something called a ZÜCA—all the kids at the rink had them. Imagine a locker on wheels: rolling luggage but sportier. I developed a system to make sure everything had its own compartment in the ZÜCA, streamlined and simple.

As ice skaters, we already have plenty of external challenges. Simply getting out on the ice is one of them. Unlike most youth sports, skating isn't taught or practiced in school. You have to do it before and after school, and you have to find a rink that has available ice time, which is limited and expensive. Ice time is precious. That's why Sherri was always so strict; we didn't have the luxury of horsing around.

More and more, competitive skaters (like Michelle Kwan and Tara Lipinski—my idols, who I grew up watching and reading about) were no longer enrolled in traditional schools, instead hiring tutors so they could practice more regularly and travel to exhibitions and competitions throughout the year. Someone like Kristi Yamaguchi—my childhood hero—was becoming the exception. Kristi, who won an Olympic gold medal in 1992, graduated from Mission San Jose, a public high school in our shared hometown of Fremont.

My parents and I began talking about my dreams, including the best way to achieve them. I was winning local competitions, and Gilley and Sherri both said that to become competitive on a national level, which was what I was wanting more and more, sacrifices had to be made. Already, the family alarm clock was set before dawn, and homework was my regular lunch-table companion—but it still wasn't enough.

You might recall my fifth-grade homeroom teacher, Mrs. Mead. At this point, she and my mom started discussing the possibility of homeschooling me. By now my passion to skate and my dream to pursue mastery of my craft were well known. Even if I didn't speak much, my actions did. I didn't ask myself if I could be an elite skater—I believed I could be one. So I asked *how* to become an elite skater, what other sacrifices I had to make. Mrs. Mead told my mom that I was an engaged, accountable student and that my math skills were solid. But she wanted to see my writing and grammar improve if I were to be removed from a formal classroom environment.

The bar was set, and I knew I had to reach it.

I committed the rest of the fifth-grade school year to becoming better at building ideas into sentences and allowing my imagination to show stories on paper. If improving my writing and grammar was what I needed in order to transition to homeschooling and commit myself wholly to skating, then that was what I would do.

At the end of the year, when I got back one of my last writing assignments, I smiled and breathed a sigh of relief when I read Mrs. Mead's note on the cover: *This is a model paper.*

Fifth grade turned out to be the last year of public school for me. It was scary leaving school: I didn't want to abandon my friends or the life I knew. But I also really wanted to focus on skating and was willing to make that sacrifice. Plus, now I wouldn't have to get up as early to skate!

From then on my daily routine was completely scripted, arranged almost as methodically as my skating programs. The weekly schedule of skating, schoolwork, and supplementary off-ice work (like stretching or ballet) provided the necessary rhythm to keep me going. I'd wake up early because I wanted plenty of time to move around, eat breakfast, and look at my phone before leaving for the rink. Once I got on the ice, the order of the day moved like so: skate a couple of hours, back home for lunch and schoolwork, then back on the ice for another two hours. I finished the training day with whatever supplementary off-ice work was necessary. At night, I made sure my schoolwork was done and in order, and then I got ready to do it all again the next day.

CHAPTER 7

WILLING TO WIN

I DON'T CONSIDER THAT FIRST COMPETITION back when I was six as the start of my journey as a competitor—that wouldn't happen until a few years later. When I won the 2010 Central Pacific Regional, I was eleven years old, and *that's* when I realized I could be competitive and would be competitive. It was thrilling! Winning regionals that October qualified me for my first major national competition, the US Junior Championships, which are held every December. I was competing as a juvenile, the youngest level. Going in, I didn't have any expectations because I was still polishing and perfecting my techniques, including the tricky double axel. Judges assess skaters' programs based on the technical elements and the difficulty of those technical elements, plus the quality of the skaters' overall skill. For actual competitions, judges give programs two scores. The first score grades the technical elements and execution; the second score is based on artistic expression, which is about the sureness and quality of your skating. It's one thing to complete all the required elements in a program. It's another to set yourself apart by having flawless innovation and footwork, which can be turns and freestyle moves. Creative, complex footwork makes a good program great.

Now, when it comes to competitions, every competitive skater must learn to execute six types of jumps, which are divided into two categories: toe jumps and edge jumps.

At the start of a toe jump, a skater buries her toe pick into the ice and uses that point like a pole vault to lift into the air. Toe jumps include the toe loop, the flip, and the lutz (my favorite). Edge jumps require a skater to use the edge to gain traction and power for takeoff, and they are the Salchow, loop, and axel (which is the most difficult jump of all). The axel is unique because it's the only jump that begins with a forward approach. With the other jumps, you enter them backward, which actually helps you gain speed for the takeoff. Preparation differs for each jump, but your landing and your in-air position—how you tightly tuck your body for the necessary rotations—are the same for all jumps.

The double axel is the hardest element required at the juvenile level, and I didn't have one in my program yet. Still, I qualified for the final round of juvenile nationals. I skated pretty well in both my short and long programs, and I ended up in fourth place. I wasn't at the top of the podium, and I hadn't expected to be, because the other girls were older than I was and they had double axels and I didn't.

Following my fourth-place finish at nationals, I felt like I should set clear goals for myself, especially since I was moving up to intermediate the next year. I wanted to be able to say I was the champion of something—that was my big goal. And each day I had to make sure I was working toward it.

Gilley had a goal and purpose for every practice session, which helped me focus on smaller goals on my way to achieving my big championship vision. One of those goals was to clean up and execute that vexing double axel. The key was leaning on the fundamentals I'd learned as a little kid. I practiced however and wherever I could. Jeffrey was such a good sport: we had toys in our shared playroom, but that playroom was also my home practice room, and I had to clear out all the toys and games to make space. Wearing these special indoor shoes, I could practice jumps. My mom would set up the video camera and record me practicing the double axel. After a few jumps, I'd ask her to stop, and we'd rewind and watch. Again and again.

"How many more turns do I need?"

"How much more?"

"How far off am I?"

My intermediate season kicked off in 2011 and started in nearby Santa Rosa with a showcase skate. I really liked the rink there. It's a Snoopy-themed rink, and I think Charles Schulz had even been there before. There's a museum right next to the rink, and Snoopy and his friends are painted all over the Zamboni. Since this was a showcase and not a true competition, it was more of a tune-up, an opportunity to work through nerves and feel the spotlight without the fear and fright of being judged. It wasn't about technical ability: you could do jumps and spins; you could skate to whatever music you wanted. It was an opportunity to explore your artistic side.

My short program was ready for the intermediate season, and I couldn't wait to debut it. I loved performing it because I loved the music: the main theme from "On Golden Pond." (Sound familiar? This marked the beginning of my love for that song.) When I'm skating to that music, trying to be like a bird, I aim to express myself with my feet, arms, and hands—with every movement of my body.

Skating like a bird and wearing a sparkly white dress, I won my showcase. I also got recalled that same night! Being recalled means you get the opportunity to skate your program again and are eligible to win a special award. I knew I probably wouldn't win the overall award, but there was a special award for choreography that I really wanted to win. That award was about a skater's complete performance persona, how she links and transitions the technical moves, as well as costume, hair, and musical interpretation.

When they announced the winner of the choreography award, they called out another girl's name. My stomach sank and my throat ached. I was disappointed. *How come she won, and I didn't? What could I have done better—what could I do better in the future? I could have won. . . .*

I stewed all the way home.

Later that night, I told my mom, "You know, it's just an award. I'm going to win nationals, and that's even better."

Looking back, I can't believe I was so brash and utterly confident that I blurted out a statement like that! As a kid, whatever I saw, whatever I wanted, I just said it and I did it. And that was that.

CHAPTER 8

GETTING OUT OF MY OWN WAY

EVERY COMPETITIVE SKATER—REALLY, EVERY competitive athlete—possesses mental toughness because they work at it. Each day is like a puzzle where you're trying to figure out how to make those butterflies in your stomach work together to be a help rather than a hindrance. It requires concentration to control the body, mind, and emotions. And the mind—I was learning— was the most important. Anytime we fall, we've already fallen in our minds before our bodies even come close to hitting the ice. The best skaters compete against themselves to overcome internal and external forces. Kristi

Yamaguchi, for instance, used her shy, quiet exterior to conceal ruthless inner drive and strength.

In 2011, one year into my competitive journey, I experienced firsthand just how strongly the mind can affect the body. And it was a near disaster.

For the second straight season, I won the Central Pacific Regional (this time as an intermediate), and in doing so I qualified for the US Junior Championships, which were being held in Salt Lake City, Utah. This is no longer the case, but back when I was younger, skaters from each region would advance to nationals and then had to qualify to make the final round, where they competed for the national championship.

The intermediate qualifiers were randomly divided into two groups: Group A and Group B. We started with about forty kids between the two groups, and the top ten would make the final based on their performances in their long programs.

I messed up big-time in my long program. I fell, and the whole thing was nerve-racking. I remember sitting in the stands afterward and regretting the whole day. *How did this happen? I can't believe this happened! What if I don't qualify?* Meanwhile Sherri and my mom were together near the ice, watching my competition execute their programs. They were so frantic that Gilley couldn't handle it and he walked away. His nerves were already frayed, and being around them only made it worse. We were all help-less as we watched the other skaters, who now controlled my fate. Only the top ten girls would advance to compete for the national title. With each performance, my name dropped on the scoreboard. Lower and lower.

Finally, after what felt like an eternity, the last skater was finished. I looked up and found my name. I was in tenth place.

I'd made it. I'd survived.

As soon as we learned I'd made the cut, we went to find another rink in town where I could practice and skate. I was really upset with my disastrous skate, and I was anxious to work those kinks out of my system. Snow had covered the ground, and my parents insisted we take a walk before I got to work.

My mom encouraged me to relax. She encouraged me to draw.

I knelt down and, with my fingertip, started to draw figures into the snow. A bunny, a bird, a mouse. Those finger strokes in the fluffy snow helped me let go and release the bad memories of my earlier performance.

I was relieved to have a second chance, and the next day, before I began my short program, Gilley reassured me, "Act as if you've just now started the competition. Be confident."

Then there was my dad, who sometimes said outrageous things to break the tension and make me laugh. "So what if you fall on your face? You won't die."

"Daddy, that's not funny."

"Whatever happens, it's okay," he continued. "We'll always be proud of you. No matter what."

I don't remember being nervous when I skated out to start my short program—unlike my mother, who was so anxious she hid behind my dad's back, barely able to turn her eyes toward the rink.

I was in the fourth and final group to skate my short program because my regional qualifying score had been among the highest. To create the birdlike imagery on the ice for "On Golden Pond," I reached back into my childhood and drew on what I'd learned in Chinese dance classes. Instead of thinking about my nerves or the pressure, I focused on how much fun I was going to have. Some of the most difficult elements of the program came during the final seconds. The tricky one-footed step work and my closing layback spin required that I keep my concentration. My mind couldn't wander and think about what-ifs or what-happened-alreadys.

Thankfully, I did not fall. In fact, I did very well! And my short program score put me in second place, just 0.01 points out of the lead. By time I took the ice to skate my long program, everyone else had skated. I knew the rankings. I knew exactly what score I needed to claim the title. I knew if I executed my program, which had multiple triple jumps and a challenging three-jump combination, the score should take care of itself.

I was fighting and attacking the program. I skated like I had something to prove. When I uncurled out of my closing spin, I waved, bowed, and scooted off the ice. I wanted to see my scores.

In the kiss and cry area off the ice, where skaters and coaches wait for marks to be revealed, Sherri had one arm around my shoulder and Kleenex in her other hand. When they announced my score, Sherri gasped and then cried. I had won the national title with the highest intermediate-level score ever awarded!

That whole experience was very surreal for me. In Salt Lake City I experienced the lows and the highs associated with competition. And after I won the title, I even signed my very first autograph. I didn't know what to sign, or how to sign—so I just wrote my name.

CHAPTER 9

MEETING A MENTOR

NOT UNLIKE THE TALES SURROUNDING URBAN legends, my skating friends and I grew up hearing stories about Kristi Yamaguchi and how she sometimes popped into one of the local California rinks without warning. Whether it was in Fremont, San Jose, or Oakland, every now and again she'd walk in unexpectedly and skate for a bit.

Growing up, I was always waiting for that moment when Kristi would miraculously show up at the rink where I was skating. After I won the intermediate title, the people at Sharks Ice wanted to make a banner for me to commemorate my accomplishment. The day they unveiled the banner was the day Kristi Yamaguchi finally came to my rink.

When she walked in, I could barely speak. I just kept looking at her, thinking, *OMGGGGGG. It's Kristi Yamaguchi.*

It took every ounce of courage I had to ask Kristi to autograph my skate. I specifically requested that she sign my right skate because I have to land on my right foot, and I thought it would be lucky. Her autograph would give me a little extra boost whenever I needed it.

As a skater, Kristi stood out among her peers. She was competitive and fierce. You don't win the Olympics and two World Championships any other way! Like me, she is small and compact, but she was quick, powerful, and light on the ice. I admired her ability to do difficult jumps. She skated with a combination of speed and grace, which I deeply respect. She was also artistic and versatile, working with Rudy Galindo to win two national titles as a pair.

I didn't just see Kristi as a role model on the ice. Off the ice, she's generous and caring. In 1996, she started her Always Dream Foundation, which is committed to improving early childhood literacy by implementing reading programs in elementary schools throughout California, Arizona, and Hawaii. And not long after she visited my rink, Kristi asked if I would be a demonstrator at a skating camp she was hosting. Obviously I said yes. My family came, too, and we met Kristi's husband. She went out of her way to be helpful, talking to me about the ups and downs skaters experience during their careers. She also took it a step further, choosing to work with me as a mentor who not only explained challenges and opportunities but also the ways I could tap into my inner strength to pull through any situation.

No matter how old I get, I will always be grateful to Kristi for the way she influenced and guided me.

CHAPTER 10

PREPARING FOR UNCERTAINTY

I CAN BE VERY NITPICKY. AND I CAN ALSO BE VERY superstitious.

I like to put on my left skate, then my right skate, and then retie my right skate. I do it every day, even for practice. It's a habit. When I'm retying, I'm not making it tighter or looser, necessarily, but as I said, I do land on my right foot, and I like my right skate to be slightly snugger than my left. Just the tiniest difference is enough for me to notice.

Those patterns that develop as part of a routine help relieve some anxiety when it comes to competing and performing. It may have been funny for me as a six-year-old not to know what warming up was, but as I grew more serious, Sherri and Gilley even choreographed my warmups. On the ice, there is no time to waste.

"First time, every time," Gilley says. "Opening pose, hit your spins and spirals. Do your jumps. Come back when you're done." A lot of coaches and their skaters chitchat near the boards during warm-ups, but Sherri and Gilley weren't interested in that. And, as you know, I wasn't much of a talker anyway. I just wanted to go skate. I don't want any distractions at all when I warm up. I've learned through the years that warming up is very important. In order for me to skate well, I have to get ready before I even go out on the ice. I find comfort in my routine.

I had moved up the ranks as a juvenile- and intermediate-level skater, competing at junior nationals, and now that I was a novice, I would be competing at the same US Figure Skating Championships as the junior and senior skaters I looked up to and admired. The championships happen over a couple of weeks, starting with the novice division, followed by the junior, before finally crowning our senior national champions.

When I showed up in San Jose for the 2012 novice nationals, I discovered the value of building in time to prepare. For the national championships, skaters are allotted practice time slots at the show rink beginning a day or two before the competition begins. We were skating at what is now known as the SAP Center, the home rink for the NHL's San Jose Sharks. Dating back to the early days with Crystal, my programs' choreography was sketched around those colorful hockey lines. But when I pushed out onto the ice for practice that day in San Jose, the ice was blank. The normal hockey circles—the red and blue lines that marked the ice—weren't there.

Whoa. What is this? Where am I?

Sherri and Gilley and my mom were right beside the rink as I skated around, having a bit of a panic attack. I didn't want to say anything to them. *It's fine. It will be fine,* I kept telling myself. But my eyes continued cutting back to the boards, looking for their faces, for what was familiar. The only thing I could do was start skating, which helped calm my freak-out. Once I began skating, I got accustomed to the rink. The lines I was used to might not have been there, but I still knew where I was: on the ice. And I would be okay.

Since San Jose was practically in my backyard, just a few minutes south of Fremont, my family and I drove back and forth to the competition each day. My pre-skate routine began as soon as we got in the van: headphones on, music up. I was getting focused and trying not to think too much about myself or what I was about to do. Really, I needed to stay calm and not think about skating just yet. That would come soon enough.

When I'd initially practiced at the arena, I scouted out a secret, private, empty spot inside the complex where I could get into the zone. While Dad and Jeffrey parked, my mom and I quietly and quickly walked to my warm-up cove. I was still listening to my playlist, and then I asked my body to slowly and deliberately start firing. Some stretches at first, followed by light jumping. Then I switched to my competition music; for the short program, I'd decided to skate to "The Chairman's Waltz" from the *Memoirs of a Geisha* soundtrack. The movements along the cello strings—languid yet sharp and precise—instantly pushed my mind into competition mode. All at once I could see and feel the music as it flowed in and out through my arms, then through my whole body and my mind. I walked through the entire program, visualizing the complete choreography, jump techniques, and spin positions. Finally, I was ready to put on my skates. *Left skate. Right skate. Stand, jump, bend a few times. Then reach down, loosen the right knot, and retie it.*

Once it was time to compete, everything happened in a blur. I do know that I fell once during the short program, but my technical elements graded very high and my second mark, which had to do with my program's artistic merit, was also good. I was the leader after the short program going into the final day of competition, which was the free skate. In terms of my routine, the second (and last) day of competition unfolded pretty much exactly as the first. Only this time, during my warm-up it was cello strikes from Nino Rota's *The Godfather* soundtrack cueing my movements.

As I was announced—"On the ice next and representing Peninsula Skating Club in San Jose, California, here is Karen Chen!"—family and friends were there supporting me, and a few people I trained with at the rink in Fremont had even made signs. *Go Karen!* one read. *Princess Karen Chen!* read another. Of course, I didn't read them at the time—only later did I see them on the video my mom had shot.

During those first moments, weaving out and in, trying to feel the ice, I gestured to the audience and the judges as if to introduce myself: *Hello, here I am . . . and I'm ready.*

Once I reached my starting mark, I listened, waiting for the music. The song started suddenly, with a quick burst of strings, which pushed my right arm down before sweeping it across my body. And then off I went. For the next four minutes, I followed the percussive taps and string chords that provided the perfect markers to signal my switches from left foot to right foot, inside and outside edge, jumps and spins, spirals and splits. It was a lot of hard work! The absolute best, most amazing kind of hard work.

In the kiss and cry area after, I was still breathing heavily when my score was announced.

"Total score," the voice said, "one hundred forty point one seven."

I smiled a big smile full of teeth, still trying to take in air, as Sherri leaned down to congratulate me and remind me that it was my highest mark ever. In fact, 140.17 was the highest novice competition score since the new judging system was put into place at the US Championships in 2007!

After claiming the novice title, I got to stick around and skate with our local skating club during the opening ceremonies for the senior national championships. Jeffrey skated with us, too. When the performance was over, the organizers led us upstairs, where we got to pose wearing Team USA jackets. I didn't get to keep the jacket, but just trying it on gave me a lot of motivation to earn a red, white, and blue jacket of my own one day.

Not long after I won the novice title, I was also awarded a scholarship from Kristi's Always Dream Foundation. I was so grateful for the assistance the scholarship provided my family to cover training costs. Particularly because, despite my record-setting performance, I had a lot to learn. Later that summer, in 2012, I would turn thirteen—finally a teenager—which meant I'd been skating for almost nine years. That's a lot of time putting my body through stress, the daily power movements of surging and soaring, and also bending and bracing to absorb the weight every time I landed on the ice and released back into the edges. I had never done much strength training; I basically just skated and stretched. I had strengths and weaknesses and imbalances, and as my body grew and changed, the weaknesses and imbalances started calling out to me and I began to feel pain. I began to struggle. Nothing had ever bothered me like this before.

In 2013 when I moved up to compete as a junior, I continued to have quite a bit of knee pain. Every day I had to wrap ice packs around my leg. I finished second in the Pacific Coast Sectional to qualify once again for the national championships, and throughout the week of nationals in Omaha, Nebraska, the ice bag was a constant training companion. When all the skaters were called together to draw for our skating order, it was right after my practice session and I walked in with ice hugging my leg. Everyone looked at me.

I'm fine. Everything is fine.

Truthfully, though, everything was not fine. I didn't understand what my body was trying to tell me. I was concerned and confused. My feet had gotten bigger, which meant my blades had, too. My legs looked almost a foot longer, and they had begun to curve with muscle. Skating can be awkward enough without your body sending you mixed messages.

Competitive skaters consciously build their seasons to peak at the right time. That's why we jam our schedules with travel and competitions at smaller rinks all over the country: we use those opportunities to practice and make sure we're correctly building to the big moments. And for all of us, one of those big moments is the national championships. Going into 2013 junior nationals in Omaha in January, I wasn't sure if all the pieces would finally come together. I loved my music and the silky, satiny, shimmery blue dress I was planning to wear for the short program. But that was where the positives ended. My wavering confidence about my changing body affected my jumps, which weren't as fluid as they used to be.

I ended up in third place after the short program, and then I stumbled on my first combination during the long program. Which meant that, in the end, I finished fourth overall.

But if I thought that was the end of big changes in my life, I was wrong.

Gilley had to have a hip operation, and he decided he could no longer travel for competitions. As my performance schedule grew more intense, I needed a coach who could always be there with me on the road. And Gilley and Sherri trained as a pair, which meant I was losing Sherri, too. My family and I had to find a new coach.

Where would I train? Where would I skate?

CHAPTER 11

BREAKING THROUGH

THE TINY STICKER ON THE SLIDING GLASS DOORS leading into Icetown offered a not-so-subtle warning: *Enter at your own risk.* This rink—buried in the corner of a strip mall, next door to a police station—was not kidding around.

Even though it was only a six-hour drive south from where I was born and raised, Riverside, California, was practically a foreign land to me. In contrast to the glowing clouds and shimmering blue bay of my childhood in Fremont, Southern California's scorched, dusty brown mountains became the scenery of my teenage years. Summers in Riverside feel like you're standing in front of an open oven, or like you just turned on a hair dryer and pointed it at your face.

But we didn't choose Riverside because of the landscape, the weather, or the rink. We chose Riverside because of Tammy Gambill.

I had first met Tammy in 2011, the summer before my intermediate year, when I went to Riverside to train with her for a week. It was like a camp where you learned new things and then went back home and took those new skills with you. Tammy grew up as a skater, but instead of dreaming of podiums, she always wanted to be a coach. She's been named developmental coach of the year by US Figure Skating multiple times, and I believed she could help me tighten up my jumps and overall techniques. Plus, Tammy had a no-nonsense reputation. I've always taken my ice time very seriously, and on Tammy's rink, she commanded everyone's focus.

So, two years later, in early 2013, when I had to find a new full-time coach, Tammy was the logical choice. But even though Tammy wasn't a complete stranger to me, the whole thing was still scary. I was leaving home for this new place, and every part of it was unfamiliar— the rink, the locker room, the benches where I'd sit and change into and out of my skates, where I'd keep my bag. Everything would be new—including me. It was weird. Which made having Jeffrey by my side even more meaningful. When my parents and I met with Tammy to agree on our coaching plan, Jeffrey was just hanging there in the background until I told Tammy that he was also a skater. "Oh my gosh, he skates!" Tammy said, before asking Jeffrey to pose for a picture. She sent it to her coaching friends all over the country with the message, *Look who arrived with Karen Chen: the cutest little boy with a huge smile!*

For the first few months as we transitioned to Riverside, Mom, Jeffrey, and I lived out of a hotel. We wanted to make sure I fit in with my new training environment before committing to a house or an apartment. We had our little hotel room during the week, and after training on Friday, we'd pack up, drive six hours north back home to Fremont, and spend the weekends with my dad. We had a difficult time being away from him, and I know he had a difficult time being away from us. I was constantly aware what my whole family was sacrificing to help me achieve my dream, and never for one second did I take it for granted.

Moving my training to Riverside was a slow, careful transition for me. Not unlike, I imagine, how many teenage girls feel when they move up into high school. At my rink in Fremont, everyone had known me and I had know them; they made signs and cheered for me at competitions. Plus, I was one of the best skaters: big fish, little pond. But in Riverside, I was this small, shy girl surrounded by colorless walls and strange faces. There was no place to hide. It was a competitive environment, and I had to figure out who my friends were and not get caught up in drama or gossip.

Most days, Mom, Jeffrey, and I went to the rink, practiced with Tammy, and barely socialized. Jeffrey and I pretty much talked exclusively to each other, and when it was time to take a training break, we went outside together, sat on the sidewalk, and ate our snacks. I usually packed fruit and yogurt, and mostly he did, too, but he also ate plenty of junk food, including his favorite, hot Cheetos.

Because I felt that skating was my job, I didn't see my new situation as a sacrifice on my part. It was simply something I had to deal with, and make the best of, in order to reach my ultimate goal. It was one more step on my journey.

In April 2013, Tammy traveled with me to my first international competition, the Gardena Spring Trophy in Italy. I won the novice division, which was, in itself, very exciting! Maybe even more exciting was when Tammy took my photo with Italian skater Carolina Kostner, the World champion and Olympic medalist.

Later that summer, I was invited to compete on the

international Grand Prix circuit as a junior. The circuit is based on your place and your points—how you finish one competition determines whether you qualify for later ones. My second international competition ever was in Latvia, and I definitely did not skate my best. I was still figuring out the rhythm and flow of international competition: I was competing on a more intense stage, plus I was jet-lagged the entire time. I took the bronze medal in Latvia, so in order to make the Junior Grand Prix Final, I knew I had to win my next event, which was only two weeks later. As soon as I got home from Latvia and shook off the jet lag, I was on a plane again, this time headed to Kosice, Slovakia. I knew I had to win, and I also knew that I was capable of winning as long as I skated clean. I was way more prepared for this second Junior Grand Prix (JGP) competition compared to the messy one in Latvia. The key was to block out the doubts in my head and allow my body to execute each jump the way I do the majority of the time in practice.

At the competition in Slovakia, I knew what to expect, and I had a better sense of exactly what I wanted to accomplish and how I would do it. I succeeded in skating two clean programs and I won the 2013 JGP Kosice!

The victory also qualified me for the Junior Grand Prix Final, which was being held in Japan, where the fans go crazy. They appreciate quality skating, and as a competitive skater, you dream about those kinds of stages. I desperately wanted to skate well for this Japanese audience.

Settling in for the plane trip from Slovakia back to California, I was finally able to take in the enormity of the moment. I was proud of my victory and excited for the opportunity ahead of me.

"You know what, I'm going to make sure I skate really well at this competition," I promised my mother before we even landed back home in the United States. "I'm going to be in my best shape ever."

Little did I know that was one promise I couldn't keep.

CHAPTER 12

FIGHTING BACK

ONE THING ABOUT THE ICE HAS ALWAYS PER-plexed me. I spend enough time on it that it's practically my second home, and truthfully, it's where I *do* feel at home. It's where I'm my best self, where I gain speed, find power, and take flight. And yet the ice is also where I can feel the most alone. When those big stages appear, and it's only me in the spotlight and everyone watching and waiting, I am isolated and alone. No one can help me. When I feel that way, I reach up and touch my jade necklace. My mom said it would protect me. But there have been times when my jade necklace wasn't enough.

✧ ✧ ✧

I poured everything into my training when I returned home at the end of the summer from the 2013 Junior Grand Prix circuit. Basically it was a countdown until the final in Japan, which started the first week of December, and I had to buckle down and streamline my schedule, eliminating distractions like mindless YouTube surfing.

The triple toe loop can give me fits, especially as part of a jump combination. It was the only technical aspect of my program that needed attention and polish. Tammy was the coach and the expert, but her advice wasn't clicking with me on this move. I had trouble understanding the concept—how Tammy was teaching and instructing me through the jump phases, how to approach and prepare for takeoff. The technique felt awkward, like I was writing with the wrong hand. My body simply didn't want to be put in that position.

I was faced with a dilemma, and I didn't know what to do. Tammy's approach to teaching skaters how to execute the triple toes had worked for everyone else, it seemed, and I didn't feel I could question her. With my past coaches, whatever they told me to do, I skated off and did it. In the van driving to the rink, I expressed my concern to my mom. "She's the coach. Maybe I'm wrong, but something doesn't feel right." I was grateful to have my mom there to nod and listen, a protective presence like the necklace I wore.

Everything came to a head on a Friday. It was the end of a long, tiring training week, and it was my mom's birthday, the twenty-seventh of September. The Grand Prix Final was in sixty-nine days. I was expecting it to be a good day: I was breaking in new skates, and I'm great in new skates because I prefer that stiffer boot. It was going to be ideal for my jumping lesson with Tammy as we worked through the new combinations.

Often on the strange new circle of ice in Riverside, I would feel for my necklace, the two tiny green beads knotted below the quarter-size piece of jade. The soft red string on my lucky jade necklace was wearing thin. After all, I'd worn it ever since my mom put it around my neck when I was nine. That particular Friday I grasped for the beads, only to feel them slip between my fingers and roll away on the ice. I held on to the jade stone, before it, too, slipped away and shattered.

I had been telling myself for weeks, *Find some new red thread, Mommy can fix it.* But I kept forgetting and never bothered to do anything about it. Now I was paying the price. I had broken what was there to protect me. *Keep going anyway. Keep pushing,* I told myself.

The thing was, deep down I knew something was truly wrong, something bigger than the necklace. I had been having some ankle issues and was experiencing random pain. But I was trying to prove myself in this still-foreign practice setting, trying to learn Tammy's style and build our trust. The last thing I felt I could do was say no or take a break. Not to mention that the countdown to competition was on, and there was no time to waste or wallow. I had to keep jumping. Even if it felt weird. Even if my good-luck charm was lost on the surface of the rink. Even if I was tired.

The lutz is the first jump in the combination and my favorite jump of them all. I tap my toe and dig the toe pick into the ice for the lift I need into the air. This time, I tapped weird, and my ankle twisted underneath me. Instead of flying through the air, I found myself sitting on the ice as a warm, sharp pain boiled down in my foot and erupted up through my right leg.

Tammy skated over to me. I was still sitting there. I didn't understand what was happening. Normally, I can talk through the pain until it goes away. *I'm fine, I'm fine. Everything is fine.*

"Give me a second. I'll get back up," I told Tammy. But I couldn't. I couldn't get up off the ice. She squatted down, supported me under my shoulders, and skated me to the boards. My right side crumpled if I tried to put any weight on it.

We unlaced my right skate, and I took my foot out. I figured if I could just stretch it, move it around, the pain would subside. But when I tried to put my boot back on, my right side recoiled, a natural reflex, almost a defense mechanism. Despite what I was telling myself—*I am fine, this is normal*—my body said differently. It was too painful to lace up my boot. That's when I knew: *I am not okay.*

My mom celebrated her birthday by driving us back home to Fremont. What was normally a six-hour drive took nine hours because we had to keep stopping to refill the bucket of ice that held my aching right foot. I breathed shallowly in and out, trying to avoid a full-blown panic attack. I was terrified. *Today is the worst day ever.*

An X-ray and MRI revealed the worst possible news: a tibial growth plate fracture. I was hoping I would only have to wear a boot so that I could remove the foot and treat the painful swelling with occasional acupuncture. But my doctor said that was too risky and a cast was necessary—which meant no skating for two months.

My mom was distraught. "I can't believe this is happening. Now you can't go to the final in Japan!" she kept saying. Inside, I was very sad, but outside, I leaned on my usual response: *This is going to be fine.* And, not surprisingly, I already had a plan. I was going to work ahead on my schoolwork and get assignments done early so that as soon as I could skate again, I wouldn't have that stress. And I decided to do physical therapy and a Pilates program to maintain as much strength as I could. I did that every single day. And every night, before I went to bed, I'd lie there in my quiet, dark room and visualize my jumps.

Everything is fine.

Perhaps the most unusual thing—and the hardest thing—was all the extra time I had on my hands. Regardless of all the rehabilitation work, or the special focus on getting ahead in my online studies, nothing managed to replace what I ultimately missed the most: being on the ice. When I skate, I come alive. The motion, the energy that burns my muscles, flushes my cheeks, and sears my lungs also ignites my soul. On the ice, I am purposeful, because on the ice, I find my purpose. It's not merely hour after hour of edge work or seeing how high I can jump. When I'm skating, I'm telling a story, I'm creating a feeling, I'm painting a picture.

During this difficult time, one lifesaving thing was art class. My parents had signed Jeffrey and me up for a local art class when I was seven, and we'd gone pretty much every week ever since, even when I was in the middle of training. This was not your usual art class. We were not instructed to draw exactly what we saw, nor were we instructed to use specific techniques. This class was more abstract. We would be given a topic or prompt, and then we were free to express ourselves through the work. For instance, maybe the subject was a rabbit. The teacher would show us the key elements for drawing a rabbit—the nose had to be in a specific place in relationship to the eyes so it looks like a bunny—but otherwise we were free to experiment and explore.

The creative energy I typically let out through skating found a release through my art. It's not that I expected the painting or drawing or sculpting would help me be a stronger skater when I finally got out of my itchy, tight cast. But all that time in front of the canvas did allow me moments to understand and explore who I truly was as a skater. And I started pushing the boundaries of my art in ways I never had before. I remember painting on wallpaper one time, because I wanted to see how the texture would reveal itself in the image. For another assignment, I painted my mom's favorite flowers, calla lilies, which are usually white, but for her, I painted them blue; I really liked that piece.

Then there was the day we were instructed to draw a tiger. Strong, fierce, and powerful: that's how I think of a tiger. All that aggressive energy bound up in the tiger is released on its prey when the moment is right. A tiger sees something and then pounces. No hesitation; the tiger goes for it. But in my painting, I camouflaged the tiger's intensity. I painted a purple tiger. I love that color, especially its variations like lavender or lilac; to me, it's a soothing color. A purple tiger is calm and collected on the outside, yet fierce inside. The eyes are the key: while soft and gentle on the edges, they are focused and intense in the center. As a skater, I connected to that concept. In fact, you might say that the purple tiger is my skating soul animal.

On December 10, 2013, almost three months after my right ankle broke, my doctor gave me the go-ahead to start skating again. Finally! I could get back to doing what I knew best.

But I quickly had to acknowledge that everything wasn't fine. I knew it as soon as the cast was removed. My calf was shriveled and shapeless. I was weak. I was wobbly. I had grown up on the ice, I had spent so much of my lifetime on the ice, but in that one moment, when I stepped back out there again, it was like I'd forgotten how to skate.

Since I had to miss the Junior Grand Prix Final in Japan, I wanted to get my form back in time for the 2014 US junior nationals in Boston, which were only three weeks away. I had to relearn everything, almost like I was doing it for the first time. My jumps, spins, stamina—everything had been lost. It was a struggle. I wasn't the skater who'd won an overseas competition just a few months before.

When the first week of January arrived, I hastily

made the decision to travel to Boston and compete. I ideally wanted to be somewhat presentable, but in my heart I knew I didn't have enough practices under my belt to have the necessary confidence to skate to win.

I was in fifth place out of thirteen competitors after skating the short program, which was no small feat considering my program's music, "Esperanza," was built on layers of beautiful Spanish guitar—and to skate that music properly, I had to be nimble, light, airy, and easy on my feet. During the whole routine, my coordination was off. I felt clunky, and I was in some pain. I ultimately decided to withdraw from the competition before the long program. My nature is to keep pushing, but deep down, I knew I didn't need to be skating. And once she saw my pain after the short program, Tammy all but insisted I withdraw. "We're not doing this," she said.

My season had ended in disaster, and the thought of returning to that rink in Riverside, to fully rehab and relearn how to skate, made me queasy. I didn't want to step back on that ice until I was fully recovered. I liked being coached by Tammy, but the environment was something else, like a high school clique no one had invited me into. At that point in my life, I didn't need the added stress of social drama. I told my mom, "I can't go back until I'm ready, mentally and physically." Maybe it would be a good idea to go see Gilley, we decided together. "It's not mind over matter," he'd always said, "it's the mind that matters." I needed my mind in the right place, and I needed to connect again to the basics of skating, the fundamentals and techniques I'd honed at my rink in Fremont. Gilley was the one who could help me do that.

CHAPTER 13

MAKING MY MARK

I WAS BRIEF AND TO THE POINT WHEN REPORTERS in Greensboro, North Carolina, asked me about my goals for that week's 2015 US Figure Skating Championships. It was going to be my senior-level debut, one year after withdrawing from the junior competition.

"The podium," I said.

Everyone probably thought I was insane, or delusional, or a naive little kid. But I was ready to let myself skate and see what happened. My words were true because I really believed a top-three finish was possible, never mind what the past year had wrought. Yes, I'd had to recover from a devastating injury. And yes, to build my muscle back, clear my head, and focus my intention, I'd decided to return to my home rink in Fremont for a while. You have to do what you need to in order to get your mind right.

I suppose I can understand everyone's skepticism, because it's not like they had X-ray vision; they couldn't see the fierce competitor inside me. And my results throughout 2014, as I'd worked my way back from the broken foot, hadn't demonstrated that I was ready to win. I'd had silver- and bronze-medal skates during the Junior Grand Prix circuit, but since I hadn't qualified for the Grand Prix Final, I didn't earn an automatic bye into the national championships. I had entered and won the Pacific Coast Sectional—my lone victory of 2014—to qualify.

In my mind, I was using those 2014 competitions as tune-ups. I hadn't skated my best, but I'd skated pretty well as the season grew longer and I grew healthier. What no one could have known was how much confidence I gained with every skate. I loved skating both my short and long programs, and the music moved and motivated me every time. I understood the depths from which I had to climb, and I was ready to climb them. And if I skated my short program at nationals the way I'd visualized it, the way I felt the music moving through me on the ice, it would be a worthy senior-stage debut. My music

My very first Halloween costume! And a glimpse into my future—I wore a lot of Disney clothes as a kid.

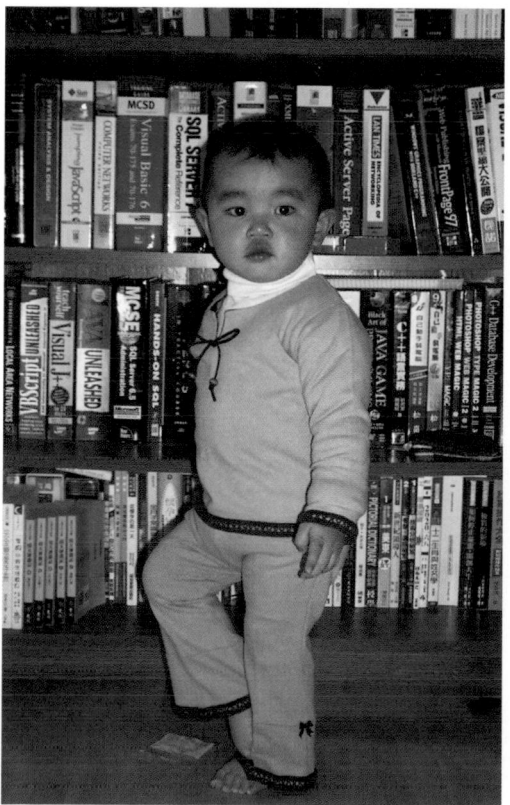

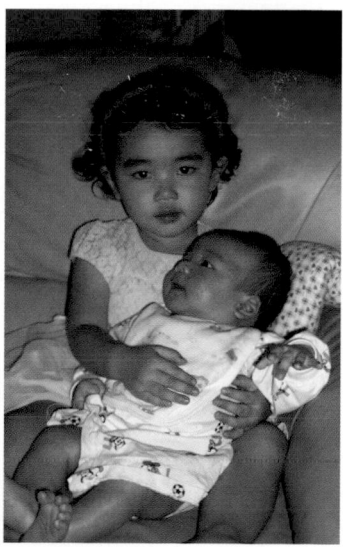

Holding my baby brother, Jeffrey.

Clearly I've liked books since the very beginning—and now I get to write one!

In one of my favorite places—my grandma's garden in Taiwan—and proud to have picked a turnip! I'm wearing yellow boots because it rains so much in Taiwan that it's always really muddy.

All smiles because I'm on the ice. I loved to flash the peace sign when I was a kid (you'll notice a theme in some of the other photos).

Skating in Taiwan and practicing a spiral. Check out my knee pads! I was always padded up.

Can't remember why I was sitting on the ice . . . I'd probably fallen. At least I'm still smiling! I always thought it was hilarious when I fell as a little skater.

Jeffrey and me. Notice, again, the peace sign (two this time!). He wore a helmet, but I refused so that people could see my hair. I always loved doing my hair in pigtails.

Dressed as the princess from *Sleeping Beauty* and holding one of my first trophies after a local competition in San Francisco.

Happy and posing for pictures with my dad. We'd just gotten home from a Christmas skating show.

Jeffrey, Mom, and me in front of the Christmas tree in our childhood home in Hayward, California.

My dad's mother and me standing on a bridge in Taiwan.

My dad's father with Jeffrey and me. That's our front yard in Hayward.

Fishing in Taiwan. I loved playing with the nets. Usually I only caught stones and pebbles: I saw plenty of fish, but was never fast enough to catch them. I spent more time getting pebbles out of my net than I did actually fishing!

With my coaches, Gilley Nicholson and Sherri Krahne-Thomas, at the 2012 US Championships in San Jose, California. I won the novice title!

Jeffrey and me, also at Nationals in San Jose. See his green bag? He brought his Nintendo DS for when he was bored watching skating. ☺

Visiting my mom's family in Taiwan.

Top row, left to right: Dad, Mom, Jeffrey, cousin Kyle. Bottom row, left to right: Uncle Steven and Aunt Trinity, my mom's younger sister; she's holding their son, my cousin Tristan (they now live in California, so I see them all the time); Grandpa; Grandma; me; Uncle Julian, my mom's brother; and his wife, Aunt Emily. My grandpa is holding Julian and Emily's son, Luis.

Our local skating club was invited to skate during the opening ceremonies at Nationals in San Jose. Jeffrey skated, too! Afterward, we posed in a photo booth wearing team jackets. It was very exciting to try one on.

My mom, me, and my mom's parents at the 2015 Audi Cup of China. It was my first international Grand Prix competition in China, and I was so excited my grandparents traveled from Taiwan to see me skate.

Jeffrey and me goofing around outside our house in Riverside, California.

My coach, Tammy Gambill, and me in the "kiss and cry" area after a national competition.

Jeffrey and I skated together for a Christmas show in Santa Barbara in 2015. We skated to "Anything You Can Do" . . . I can do better!

Enjoying family time. Jeffrey loves taking pictures of wildlife and birds. What better backdrop than the Golden Gate Bridge?

Jeffrey and me after a Christmas show in Santa Barbara in 2016.

My friends at Sharks Ice in Fremont, California, threw a party for me after I won Nationals in 2017. I was so excited Kristi Yamaguchi could be there!

choice, "Requiem for a Tower," mirrored my emotional state from the past year. Foreboding, it begins, almost like the ticking clock of a bomb. Then the strings kick in, slowly but steadily gaining power and strength. Then the restless opening gives way to a triumphant close. My footwork, jumps, and spins would harness all my energy to embody that final fearlessness and fight. With every cut of my blade, each turn on my edge, each spiral and rotation, I would skate to overwhelm the cacophony of naysayers and doubters. On the ice, with this music, my spirit would surge. I would soar.

Going into the national championships, I was the newbie. I didn't feel the pressure of expectation because virtually no one expected anything out of me. It had been a few years since I'd won the novice title as a twelve-year-old, and by now I was fifteen and shaking off rust and an injury. Luckily Tammy's strict, structured training atmosphere had helped me prepare for my senior nationals debut.

Tammy left nothing to chance. Everything was mapped out. When I arrived in Greensboro for the championships, I didn't feel anxious about the unknown. We knew how to organize my preparation and competition timeline because we'd simulated it during training. Since everything at a competition is based on skating order, at practice Tammy had her skaters draw numbers, and then we'd have a mock competition, skating in an order based on our drawn numbers. So, no matter whether I ended up the first, fourth, or sixth skater at a competition, I knew exactly how to fill the minutes while I waited because I'd done it before. For example, if I was the last skater in my group, I knew that after our group warm-up on the ice, I had time to take my skates off for a little bit, do a few more jumps to stay loose and ready, and visualize my program. Since we'd practiced virtually every possible scenario, there was no situation that was confusing or rushed. I could execute the plan without second-guessing myself.

By the time I skated out to my mark on that first day of competition at nationals, wearing my stone-studded amethyst dress and my wonderfully Mom-reinforced jade necklace, I was ready to knock the doors off this short program.

How far can I push?

You got this.

Let's go.

It was an intense two-minute, forty-second program, and the first thirty seconds I was skating out and away, pushing past the negative energy and finding my soul. I was hurtling down the ice for my first big jump, a triple-lutz, triple-toe combination. It wasn't perfect; my lutz was huge and I was still figuring out the toe, but I landed smoothly. The beauty of this music for me was how it built momentum. The longer it went, the more fun I had. Once I hit my triple loop, the double axel released out of me on instinct. From an emotional spiral to a confident spin, this program told my story. I skated my story.

Going into the final night of competition where I'd skate my long program, I was in sixth place. Again, there was no expectation from anyone except myself—but I've always been my own worst critic. Something about this program, though, gave me good feelings. I'd first skated to "The Godfather Suite" during my novice year when I won the title. But when you're a novice, programs are shorter, so I'd had to edit out some of my favorite musical sections. For my first senior long program, I had more time to fill, and I knew this music would challenge me technically and fulfill me artistically.

When my name was announced, I plowed out on the ice, absorbing the crowd in Greensboro, easily the largest and loudest I'd ever experienced. It brought a smile to my face, and I pulled in a big gulp of air to get my focus. I was ready to skate. I felt everything was working together, including my red hairpiece, the red string on my necklace, and the pops of red on the skirt of my shimmery black dress. I curved away from the starting mark, and in my ears, the ripping sounds of my blades cutting into the ice overpowered the early string notes of "The Godfather Suite." I was flying.

That speed lifted me into the first jump, a triple combination. I landed it, still a little short, but it boosted me, and I pulled off four more triples to capture every angle of edge and every ounce of speed to complete this four-minute, ten-second jumping, sweeping dance as cleanly as I'd started.

The packed crowd inside Greensboro Coliseum rose to their feet. I could barely hear Tammy's giggling as I skated over to the boards. She wrapped me in a big hug before I even stepped off the ice. In practice, she pushes me hard, and I think it's because she wants me to experience moments like that during competition.

Tammy was very pleased with my execution, and the judges agreed with her, giving me high technical marks. My two-day total was 199.79. I could barely believe it. I was in first place! That wouldn't end up lasting, but my score was good enough for me to hold on to third by the conclusion of the competition.

I made the podium behind Sochi Olympians Ashley Wagner and Gracie Gold. I took selfies with both of them.

I was proud of my bronze medal, but mostly I was proud of how I'd skated. I'd wanted the spectators to feel emotion when I was on the ice, and I know they did. I think people saw hope.

I made a serious impression in Greensboro. Just as I'd told those reporters I would, I'd made the podium, and I showed everyone that the past year was history. I was ready to move forward and chase my dream. And if I kept skating and progressing, I knew people would see me as one to watch for.

CHAPTER 14

LEARNING BALANCE

THE 2015–2016 COMPETITIVE SEASON: OTHERWISE
known as the season that never fit.

And by never fit, I mean my boots.

I know way more than I want to about skating boots.

Usually, you train with one pair of skates and then you have a backup pair as well. When your main pair starts breaking down and no longer provides the support you need, you need a new pair.

They're pretty fickle things, these skating boots, with so many things going on. The blade has to be mounted at a certain angle, which depends on the skater because we each distribute our weight differently. Skates also have a heel height, and you'd think the measurement would be consistent from one pair to the next, but that's not always the case. So, when I lace up my boots and hold my weight up on top of that sharp steel blade, a quarter-inch difference here or there can cause some big problems. In my case, those problems meant an unfortunate downhill turn after my breakout performance at nationals.

Starting in the spring of 2015, and throughout much of the next year, I ended up trying out at least twenty pairs of boots. The company that made the boots I'd been wearing most of my skating life had gone out of business, and I was struggling to find a new pair that worked for me. I tried wearing stock, non-custom boots, but those weren't comfortable. I couldn't train consistently because I was constantly in pain. I have flat feet to begin with, and then I'd broken my right ankle twice—none of which helped my boot issues. If my foot was set in a weird position, it caused severe arch pain.

The boot is important because it's what connects me to the ice. Tammy always says, "Skaters need happy feet." I want to feel stable in my boots, like they're supporting me and holding my feet in the right position. If my heel slips around or my ankle shifts, it's almost impossible to stay perfectly balanced because I can't hold my edge.

As a result of these annoying boot issues, what I had

been able to do easily a year earlier when I took bronze in my senior nationals debut, was now a chore. Spins and spirals—which had been my strengths since I was little—felt scary. Plus, there was this nagging pain all over my body. With my feet in weird positions, everything else compensated to support me, which resulted in knee pain, back pain, hip pain. Pain, pain *everywhere*.

Of all the problems my boots caused, my jumps got the worst of it. Remember how I said little things can make big differences on the ice? That's especially true with jumping. Because if you don't feel comfortable moving in your boots, you won't have the confidence to lift off into the jump. Every detail matters, like when and where and how I use my toe pick to dig into the ice. When I manage to get the timing of everything just right, the ice actually launches me into the air. It's like I'm defying gravity; there's no rush quite like it.

Jumps are the central focus of figure skating these days, and while every individual has her own style and strengths, jumps have four specific phases: preparation, takeoff, rotation, and landing. Timing is what connects those phases together. During the preparation, I make sure I have the rhythm I need to launch explosively from my knees into takeoff. In the air, I want to be straight head-to-toe, with tight arms and tight legs. Tammy says to try to scratch my back as I wrap my arms around myself. And then for the landing, grab the ice with the toe of the blade, and extend out. Tammy is strict about landing positions, and the finish and polish you add to the jump. She says jumps are like a storybook. The "once upon a time" is the setup, the story is in the air, and a great landing means they lived "happily ever after."

The axel and lutz are considered two of the most difficult jumps, and ironically, they're my two favorites. For both, you land on the right outside edge, and I've always had a natural thing for the outside edge. The lutz is uniquely difficult because I launch into it with my right toe tapping the ice while also holding to the left outside edge. My body goes from spinning one way to another in a split second, but for some reason, my body has always wanted to do that jump.

I tried so many crazy things to find a solution to my boot issue. I tried wearing one brand of skate on my left and another on my right. In August when I went to to Champs Camp, a performance-based simulation camp at the Olympic Training Center in Colorado, I even tried wearing my brother's skates. There I was, performing my short and long programs for the season, getting feedback from judges, and I'm rocking black skates. I got some pretty weird looks.

That year, it was a struggle to get my body to do anything. Everything was out of sync and disconnected. I selected Puccini's "Nessun Dorma" for my short program and selections from *Les Misérables* for the long program. Those pieces are intensely dramatic, beautiful, and meaningful. They unravel at slower paces, taking time to tell stories that are both bold and dark. I picked these pieces because I wanted to branch out and push myself to be a more mature skater. I believed the music would help me grow. I connected to the music emotionally but had a hard time capturing the rhythm. With slower, more thoughtful music, I had more time to think as I skated, and that often meant I was thinking about my feet trembling in my boots or worrying about my right edge slicing out away from me when I needed to land my jumps. Those thoughts can haunt you.

If you look at my results from that season, they do tell a lot of the story. It was an up-and-down ride; I only finished on the podium a couple of times and was eighth in my return to nationals. But I also competed internationally in China for the first time. My grandparents were able to come from Taiwan to watch me skate, and that was a wonderful experience.

For me, the most significant part of my story is what happened before, between, and after all those results. I was learning every step of the way. I've always been committed, as you've no doubt picked up on by now. Working with Tammy I became even more diligent in my approach to each day, which was key as a senior-level skater. The skating/training/schoolwork schedule and routine stayed the same, but I settled down and emphasized organization and structure. I knew I needed to be stable and commit to those extra details to keep my body and mind healthy. Rest is an essential part of an athlete's recovery, and my mom insisted I get to sleep by ten thirty every night. I didn't always succeed—homework, remember?—but, hey, I tried.

I also got tougher. I figured out how to take a difficult problem, like my boots not fitting, and search for the solution. Finally, after trying out dozens of different pairs, I did find a boot maker, Avanta, that could customize skates, and I discovered a pair that was comfortable for me. The great people at Avanta invested so much time toward making my feet happy again, and helped me continue doing what I love. They even named my boots: K One, K Two, K Three, and so on.

And through each of my difficult skates, I reconnected the importance of music to my performance. To skate well, I need to skate what I feel, what I know, and what I want.

So for my next season—2016–2017, the year I was determined to find my fit—I knew what I wanted. I wanted to be a champion.

CHAPTER 15

BECOMING THE DREAM

AFTER GETTING BRONZE AT 2015 NATIONALS, I'D felt I could accomplish greater things. So when I went on to finish eighth at nationals the following year, it was a huge disappointment. I had to take some time to rediscover why I was still skating, why I loved it. I decided to look back on the years when I first fell in love with skating. I watched old videos, and I watched the short program from my intermediate year. I remembered how much I loved that program and that music from *On Golden Pond*. I felt like I needed something that I was used to, something that was familiar to me, so I could focus on skating a stellar short program. At any competition, and especially at a top-level event like the national championships, strong placement after the short is necessary in order to be a contender for the podium. That means no falls and no technical mistakes. It has to be close to perfect; one small mistake would cost points, and I'd slide way down on the scoreboard.

No skater goes into a season thinking they'll do their choreography themselves. I didn't plan on it, and it was basically an accident, but I ended up doing my own for the 2017 season. At the senior level, the coaches weren't the choreographers. We usually brought in special choreographers each season, but I wanted to experiment and be in control of my own program. Most of the time, I didn't really know what I was doing. I wasn't a choreographer. I did know what technical elements are required, and I played around. I guess it was like when my mom encouraged me to draw figures in the snow that day I survived to make intermediate nationals in Salt Lake City. "It makes you relax," my mom said then. And it was still true. Now I was sketching my movement patterns in the ice.

On Golden Pond, with its soft and quiet tones, suited me. For some reason, despite my size (I'm barely five feet tall), people envisioned me as a strong and powerful skater. And I *was* a powerful skater, but I also thought I was an elegant skater. When I was a little girl in Chinese dance class, we learned the peacock dance, and through

that dance, we learned the importance of every movement. The angle of my elbow, the flick of my wrist, the
pressure and placement of my fingertips: each gesture
combined to paint a picture of a peacock.

To skate my story, I needed precision and focus. Yes,
I wanted to skate like a bird. I wanted to be a champion.
And at the senior level, a winning performance requires
not just supreme skating but also a compelling persona.
I had to look like a bird and embody a bird on the ice.
From the very moment I conceptualized my short program, I envisioned myself wearing white. I was inspired
by a picture of a snow-white peacock, whose feathers
were fanned with a regal quality. Early in the season, I
received feedback that white wouldn't stand out against
the ice and that it wasn't a "slimming" color the way black
was. So I had a second dress made, a blue one, and it was
fine, but it wasn't the bird I knew I could be. The bird I
wanted to be was white. When it was time to pack for
nationals, I didn't even put the blue dress in my suitcase.

It was my first time visiting Kansas City, Missouri, but
I felt at home as soon as I walked through the airport. I
saw these shirts in the terminal shops that said, *I Love
KC*. I joked with my dad: "KC—my initials. This is going
to be a great competition for me."

We actually arrived several days early because my

brother was also competing. Very quietly, Jeffrey had become an accomplished skater in his own right. At the Icetown rink in Riverside, a banner hangs from the rafters commemorating the pewter medal he won in 2014 at juvenile nationals. To support Jeffrey, I arrived in Kansas City on Friday night, watched him skate on Saturday and Sunday, then started practicing Monday for nationals. The senior nationals were set to begin on Thursday, the nineteenth of January.

The Sprint Center was similar to most of the arenas where we competed. The main floor, or in our case, the ice, was surrounded by a circular tunnel, and little hallways and doorways shot off from that heavily trafficked path. I planned out some time after my official practice session so I could scout the area and find my warm-up cove. First, I located a staircase and decided to follow it up. Lucky for me, it led to an open area with flooring and high ceilings. It was the perfect place.

Leading up to the competition's opening night, my practices were decent. I always found things to work on, and it was my nature to try "just one more" jump, aiming to piece together the perfect preparation, takeoff, rotation, and landing. Of course, perfection was fleeting, so I was learning to find happiness in my effort.

On opening night, I was settled and ready as soon as I stepped on board the shuttle that carried us from the hotel to the arena. I listened to my playlist through my headphones, looked out the windows, and chatted quietly with my mom, just going through my normal routine, doing all the things that helped me not think about that one very important thing: skating a clean short program.

Once I arrived at the arena, I followed the staircase. This time I knew exactly where it led. It was quiet, calm, and still. No distractions. I closed my eyes to visualize my program, to twist my body open, away and free from any nervous, tight energy bubbling inside me. First, some light and easy jumping, waking up my muscles, asking them to be loose and limber that night. Then I switched my music to that familiar sound, the song of birdcalls and piano notes—the music that reminds me who I am and what I want to do.

I want to be a national champion.

For a moment, I grew tense. Stiff. I was thinking too much.

Oh no, it's the short. You're going to screw this up. You always mess this up.

I breathed. I listened. I heard the birds. They didn't fear the ground, because they were looking at the sky.

Skate that way, Karen. You don't have to be afraid. Time to spread your wings and fly.

Finally, the warm-up was over. The visualization had ended. I left the stairwell and rejoined the intensity and noise of the arena.

Very quickly, the moment for competition arrived. My name was announced, and I took one loop around the ice, just like I'd done hundreds, probably thousands, of times before. My icy white dress rippled in the cold air, and the beading was intricate, ornate, and spectacular. Even my mom had been satisfied with it.

I circled into my mark, took one more deep breath, and then there was no more time to think. My music began, but I didn't. I waited for a couple of seconds, letting the music move me until I was ready to pour all my emotion onto the ice.

My first jump was the moneymaker: it was a combination, so the landing foot of the first jump was the takeoff for the second. This triple-lutz, triple-toe loop has forever given me fits, and I often rush the landing into the next takeoff. Not this time, though. This time I remembered my breathing, remembered to use my knees, and let myself go for it. I nailed it.

I had two more jumps left. The last one was a double axel, which was considered really easy for me. But that middle jump, the triple loop, is past the halfway point, and sometimes when I overthink or doubt myself, it won't happen. Then I started to smile, and I landed the triple loop. All my longing for this moment, and it was about to happen.

Keep going. You got this.

Stay calm.

Spin and hit the ending pose.

And I did it. I skated the way I envisioned.

It was one of the best feelings I've ever experienced. I've always had that mental block with the short program; I feared it, and to be able to skate clean, without slips or missteps, when it counted the most—I felt redeemed. I felt proud. All skaters live for that moment where we realize everything came together, all the hard work paid off, all those hours of training were worth it.

Then my score was announced: 72.82, the highest short-program mark on record at the national championships.

I was the leader after the short program. My body was shocked and full of energy. That night I had trouble falling asleep. What else could I possibly dream? I had just skated the program of my dreams.

Thankfully, we had a day in between the short and long programs, and Tammy and I were careful with my preparation to reset my mind and focus. It was certainly no time to be smug and rest on my laurels, but skating such a solid short program definitely gave me a confidence boost.

And this long program had been my favorite thing to skate all season. I'd practiced it a lot, over and over. The music, "Jealousy Tango," had a different feeling than my skates from the previous year. I chose it specifically so I wouldn't get lost thinking on the ice, dwelling on slow, depressing music.

I gave myself plenty of time to warm up because, as the leader, I had certain obligations. NBC needed to pre-record footage of me getting ready for the broadcast, so I did some jumps and spins in front of the camera, then tiptoed back up the staircase for my quiet preparation and a mini pep talk.

Clear my mind, that's what I needed to do. Some-times I think all these thoughts, and they can be positive thoughts, but I hear them over and over in my head. *I can do this. I can do this. You can do it, you can do it, You got this.* It's frantic.

When I have good skates, my mind is clear. And I just skate.

I was the third-to-last skater on the last night of com-petition. Tammy urged me one final time, "Stay hungry. Push through," before I was called to take the ice.

"In first place after the short program, joining us from the Peninsula Skating Club in San Jose, California, please welcome Karen Chen!"

What are people expecting out of me this time? What are they thinking and saying? I honestly didn't know, nor did I care. I knew what I'd come to do. I'd come to win a championship.

My focus was locked in before the bow hit the strings.

Right off the top, that first combination, the testy triple-lutz, triple-toe loop told me I was ready. I heard it as my right blade cut that happily-ever-after edge on the landing. I remained fast and sure, hitting six triple jumps and filling out the ice with spins, spirals, and glides.

When the music stopped, and I released out of the closing Biellmann spin, my hands went to my knees. The long was only a little more than four minutes, but I should have been exhausted if I'd left everything out there. And I was. I had nothing to regret.

The judges awarded me with the third-highest free skate score in competition history, and my two-program total was 214.22. Two skaters remained, but I was happy. I knew that no matter what, I had earned a medal. I had skated with my soul. I had skated my story.

Back home in California, my mom's sister watched the television broadcast while FaceTiming my grandparents in Taiwan. Thanks to the internet and two screens, they watched me skate like a peacock, like a leader, and like a winner. My family watched my dreams come true.

I want to be a champion.

That year, I finished as the national champion.

CHAPTER 16

LISTENING TO MY VOICE

I COULD HARDLY SEE. REALLY, I COULDN'T SEE AT
all. The funny thing is, not seeing was helping me focus.
Since I couldn't see the crowd, read the signs around the
rink in Helsinki, Finland, or make out any of the judges'
faces, all I could see was what I was doing.

This was my first World Championships.

I wear nighttime contact lenses and have worn them for
what feels like most of my life. In second grade, I was
struggling to see the board from my desk in the classroom, and I've needed glasses or contacts ever since.
People don't really wear hard contacts like mine anymore;

it's considered old technology, and not necessarily completely reliable, but I've been wearing them a long time, so I just continue with it. With nighttime lenses, you put them in right before bed and during the night, like magic, your vision is being corrected. So, I go to sleep and the next morning, I take them out and I can see fine throughout the day.

With hard contacts, you're supposed to replace them every year, but sometimes I waited a little too long. I finally got new contact lenses right before the World Championships, which were in late March 2017, a couple of months after my win at nationals. For some reason, the new lenses weren't working for me. I slept in them a few nights, but my vision didn't seem any better during the day. I figured, *Your eyesight isn't perfect: just deal with it. You can still skate. It will be fine.*

When I got to Helsinki and started the official practice sessions, not only could I not see well, I also had pain in my eyes. They were really uncomfortable. I had a backup pair of soft contact lenses, so I decided to try them during the next practice session. I mean, this was my senior worlds debut! I wanted to see the arena, the walls, everything! So I put in my backup contacts and was instantly overwhelmed. Finally I could see everything, including all the faces sitting in the stands, watching my practice, not to mention all the cameras aimed at me.

Everything was so bright, shifting in and out of focus. I got dizzy. And I skated horribly.

Off the ice, I nearly had a breakdown. What was happening? I was the national champion, and I was crumbling again.

Worlds were no small amount of pressure, because the scores of the top two finishers for US skaters had to add up to no more than thirteen to guarantee our country three Olympic bids for the coming year.

In the end, I would basically have to skate blind; I would have to skate without anything to correct my terrible vision. Instead, I would skate on feel and instinct, the best way to skate. Or, as my mentor Kristi Yamaguchi told me before the competition, "Skate dumb." What she meant was: stop thinking so much. And I'm kind of thankful, actually, that I had such a hard time with my contacts, because it forced me to block everything out and put all my focus and intention toward performing and competing—exactly what Team USA needed me to do.

After the short program, I was fifth and my United States teammate Ashley Wagner was seventh. At most competitions, I didn't allow myself to watch my competitors or even know how they skated and scored. It was better if I focused on myself. In reality, that wasn't always possible. That day, before I started my long program, I did happen to see the jumbotron, and I knew that Ashley hadn't skated as well as she'd wanted or as well as I knew she was capable of. Getting those three spots at the Olympics would be challenging, and it all depended on how I skated that day.

Now, what most people don't know, what I've never told anyone before, is that I suffer from a chronic, and at times debilitating, back condition. My whole life, I'd been able to stretch and I was very flexible, especially in my back, which helped me execute spins and spirals from a very young age. Then, a few years ago, sometime after I broke my foot that day in Riverside, this back injury flared up. I've seen many doctors for it, and I've gotten different opinions. Some say I was born with the problem, others say I must have had an accident when I was younger that triggered it. Basically, my lower vertebrae sometimes slip forward and backward because the bones are slightly cracked. When I arch my back in certain ways, bone pushes against nerve, and pain shoots down my legs and back. I've had doctors tell me not to arch my back, but I have to arch my back in order to compete and execute certain moves. So you can see my dilemma.

When I was initially diagnosed, I was so worried about my spine and so nervous about the pain that I was tense all the time. And that tension made everything worse. I was tight and my muscles were constantly seizing, which only intensified the sharp pain radiating from my back down through to my legs.

I decided I needed to be careful and play it safe, not pushing it so far that even normal activities would hurt my back. In training, when I'd run through my programs, I only performed basic movements. For example, if it was a spiral, I wouldn't lift my legs as high. I toned everything way down.

As you know, I managed to win bronze at nationals in 2015. But my performances grew more and more inconsistent. How could I expect myself to hit positions in competition if I never did them in practice? That's not how athletes train. Training halfway is not the proper way to train. *I'm being lazy.*

Finally I had to have a conversation with my doctor. "You have this problem," he said, "but worrying about it won't make it better. And arching your back isn't going to make it any worse."

Champions figure out a way to persist. And in order to help my back, I added more Pilates and core stability work to my off-ice training. All those core muscles help hold my vertebrae in position. If my core was strong, the vertebrae weren't as likely to slip around and cause further problems.

Initially, my back pain was scary and I dealt with a lot of fear. But my only choice was to figure out a way to overcome the fear. I tried avoiding it—which didn't work. It was only after I embraced it that I found a breakthrough. My back condition forced me to strengthen other areas of my body, which made me more powerful overall. In my weakness, I found strength.

So there I was, in cold and dreary Finland, in the best skating shape of my life, but blind as a bat, with the pressure of the world literally settling down on my shoulders for my long program. How would my back hold up?

Within thirty minutes, I told myself as I got psyched up for my long, *we'll know what's going to happen*.

And just like that, I was calm.

That day I skated dumb. I didn't skate perfectly or even completely clean, but I skated the way I like to: fast and free. I did mess up a couple of jumps; my spins, however, were strong and gave me enough points to make up for the slips. I finished in fourth place for the United States and helped secure three roster spots for our country at the 2018 Winter Olympics!

In the greenroom, where the top-ranked skaters wait and see how the rest of the field scored, I took a seat next to Carolina Kostner. I didn't know it at the time, but

Tammy took a photo of me sitting with Carolina. Tammy surprised me after the competition, showing me that photo alongside the one I'd pleaded for her to take with Carolina more than three years ago, when I was barely a junior skater. "Oh my gosh, there you two are again," Tammy said. "And now you're competing against her."

I was grateful Tammy used that moment to make me acknowledge how much I'd grown over the past few years. I'd grown as a skater and as a competitor, and I'd learned more about myself and who I was. And, perhaps most difficult of all, I'd learned what I could handle.

Sometimes it takes a while to process difficult situations. And it's perfectly fine to be patient with yourself, so long as you commit to the process and figure out the next step.

I write myself notes to stay motivated. One time, I wrote, *Two weeks from now, you'll thank yourself.* That time in my life was a difficult stretch of training, and I wasn't getting anything right. But I knew if I just persisted, it would pay off.

Ultimately, my only successes in the first half of that 2017 season were at nationals and at worlds. Fortunately, if you're going to do well at two competitions, those are two good ones to choose! Everything else, though, was me figuring my way up. I was tested constantly, and through skating I was learning how to confront different emotions, struggles, and obstacles and how to deal with them all.

It's almost like trial and error. Sometimes, there are those days when I don't feel it, when I don't feel very motivated emotionally. Those are the days I need to push myself. But there are also days when my body actively doesn't feel good, and mentally it's a struggle to know how to work hard in the face of the pain.

I'm still learning and trying to figure out what works and what doesn't.

CHAPTER 17

CONTINUING THE JOURNEY

I GUESS MY STORY DOESN'T REALLY HAVE AN END-ing. Certainly not yet.

No matter what, no matter what I achieve or how hard things get, no matter how many triple axels I land or edges I catch, I'm going to keep trying.

When I found skating, I discovered my joy. I couldn't wait to get to the rink and go skate. It was pure fun. I never wanted to stop, and as I kept working at it, as I was competing more, I gradually noticed I was getting better. I started allowing myself to set goals.

I want to accomplish this, and this, and this.

I want to be able to do this jump soon, and so I'd work at it.

I'd do it over and over and over.

In a way, I say to myself, *We'll see how this goes.* Because the training, the everyday skating, that's what I really love: the process. Of course, I have good memories and bad memories, as well as ups and downs. I've learned all my life that I do hope and dream for all these things, but sometimes what I imagine as the road to accomplishment ends up being completely different than I expected.

I've learned to accept that sometimes you can't always achieve your goal. So you move on and set new goals.

Sometimes, the struggle is necessary. Each day presents its own challenge. During those tough moments, we build up our strength and perseverance. We discover who we are, and what's worth the fight.

Skating, above all, has made me a fighter. Skating teaches me to believe in myself.

When I watched Olympic champion Evan Lysacek skate to "El Tango de Roxanne" from the movie *Moulin Rouge* during the Smucker's Skating Spectacular at the 2011 US Championships, I instantly fell in love with that music. Ever since then, I've always wanted to skate to it. In the back of my mind, though, I told myself that I couldn't live up to the music's intensity. I never brought it up. I never told anyone.

Fortunately, and unfortunately, it was a huge struggle for me to find the right music for my short program for the 2017–2018 season, especially with 2018 being an Olympic year. I needed music that would provoke my emotion on the ice so I could develop a bold program. Or, as Tammy would say, something fierce. Out of desperation, I decided to put it out there, this idea of choosing "El Tango de Roxanne" for my music. Surprisingly, everyone loved the idea! And thus my short program for 2017–2018 was born.

My long program is to *Carmen Suite* after Bizet's opera, by Rodion Shchedrin. Originally I was going to skate to *Tosca*. However, even after the program was choreographed, there was never a spark. I felt the need to find something better, something that motivated me. And that's when I came across *Carmen*. At first I was skeptical, but I really felt that I could make this special and interpret it my way so that it would be my own version of *Carmen*.

I'm still learning. I'm still learning to trust my instincts and make the right decisions. I certainly don't have all the answers. But if I could recommend just one thing, one little thing to strive for each day, I'd tell you to get lost in the moment. Be so consumed with what's happening here, in the present, that the whispers of doubt are nothing but background noise. When I focus on the very next step, on what is directly in front of me, it releases me from worry. If I'm concentrating on what I'm doing— what I can control—then I'm not imagining worthless scenarios that may or may not happen.

What I remember the most from my art classes is there was no right or wrong answer, as long as we completed the work and had fun. The teacher gave us the materials and the topic, but we were free to do whatever we wanted. I focused on putting color on the canvas, creating whatever image I held in my heart. I felt safe to try anything because I knew the finished product wasn't going to be judged. What mattered was the effort I put into making it.

I feel that way when Jeffrey and I are together on the ice. It doesn't happen as much anymore, because he's training as an ice dancer now, and our lives are busy, but we still manage to goof off from time to time. Skating with Jeffrey, I always feel confident to try things I otherwise wouldn't, like tracing the figure of a tiny heart over and over again. That's how I started to love skating. I pushed out on the ice, and every time, it was new. Nothing seemed silly or stupid. I was learning, growing, and discovering. Yes, there were right and wrong ways to execute the techniques, but I succeeded by doing, by trying. Over and over and over again.

Skating allowed me to become an individual, because it demanded courage. For a skater, the biggest embarrassment is not sliding on our backsides across the ice. No, the worst thing we can do is back away from a challenge, give in to the fear.

Life is complicated, and it can be frustrating. Sometimes I feel like I'm working my tail off and yet I don't see results.

And that's when I remind myself, *Keep going, you got this,* because I'm not done writing my story yet.

EPILOGUE

THE OLYMPIC CREED
OF 1894

THE MOST IMPORTANT THING IN THE OLYMPIC
Games is not to win, but to take part, just as the most
important thing in life is not the triumph, but the struggle. The essential thing is not to have conquered, but to
have fought well.

CAREER SUMMARY

2017 US champion

2015 US bronze medalist

2012 US novice champion

2011 US intermediate champion

All-Time Results

2017—World Team Trophy—3rd (team)

SP: 60.33, LP: 108.62

2017—World Championships—4th (199.29)

SP: 69.98 (5), LP: 129.31 (6)

2017—Four Continents Championships—12th (166.82)

SP: 55.60 (12), LP: 111.22 (10)

2017—US Championships—1st (214.22)

SP: 72.82 (1), LP: 141.40 (1)

2016—Golden Spin of Zagreb—7th (155.63)

SP: 54.60 (6), LP: 101.03 (7)

2016—NHK Trophy—6th (178.45)

SP: 58.76 (7), LP: 119.69 (5)

2016—Cup of China—7th (179.39)

SP: 58.28 (9), LP: 121.11 (5)

2016—US International Classic—3rd (162.08)

SP: 51.50 (6), LP: 110.58 (3)

2016—Four Continents Championships—12th (161.52)

SP: 53.55 (12), LP: 107.97 (10)

2016—US Championships—8th (168.75)

SP: 54.86 (12), LP: 113.89 (8)

2015—Golden Spin of Zagreb—3rd (175.35)

SP: 56.82 (4), LP: 118.53 (8)

2015—Cup of China—5th (175.93)

SP: 58.30 (7), LP: 117.63 (5)

2015—Skate America—5th (172.54)

SP: 62.28 (4), LP: 110.26 (6)

2015—US International Classic—4th (159.18)

SP: 60.94 (3), LP: 98.24 (5)

2015—World Junior Championships—8th (157.30)

SP: 51.64 (12), LP: 105.66 (8)

2015—US Championships—3rd (199.79)

SP: 64.66 (6), LP: 135.13 (3)

2015—Pacific Coast Sectional—1st (171.58)

SP: 54.83 (2), LP: 116.75 (1)

2014—Junior Grand Prix, Croatia—2nd (169.41)

SP: 62.71 (1), LP: 106.70 (3)

2014—Junior Grand Prix, Czech Republic—3rd (160.95)

SP: 60.68 (1), LP: 100.27 (4)

2014—World Junior Championships—9th

2014—US Championships, Junior—Withdrawn

2013—Junior Grand Prix (Slovakia)—1st

2013—Junior Grand Prix (Latvia)—3rd

2013—Gardena Spring Trophy, Novice—1st

2013—US Championships, Junior—4th

2013—Pacific Coast Sectional, Junior—2nd

2012—US Championships, Novice—1st

2012—Pacific Coast Sectional, Novice—1st

2012—Central Pacific Regional, Novice—1st

2011—US Junior Championships, Intermediate—1st

2011—Central Pacific Regional, Intermediate—1st

2010—US Junior Championships, Juvenile—4th

2010—Central Pacific Regional, Juvenile—1st

IJS Personal Bests

International Competition

SP—69.98 (2017 World Championships)

LP—129.31 (2017 World Championships)
Final Score—199.29 (2017 World Championships)

US Qualifying Competition
SP—72.82 (2017 US Championships)
LP—141.40 (2017 US Championships)
Final Score—214.22 (2017 US Championships)

Career Notes

2011 Junior Nationals, Intermediate Ladies Division
Karen's score (combined short program and long program) was 119.92 points—the highest score at the intermediate level since the International Judging System was implemented in 2007. The opening Level 4 layback spin earned 4.20 points and received straight 3 grades of execution from the judging panel.

2012 US Nationals, Novice Ladies Division
At age twelve, in her debut at the US Figure Skating Championships, Karen captured the novice ladies title with 140.17 points, the highest competition score recorded in the current judging system. Her margin of victory was 14 points.

2017 US Nationals

At age seventeen, Karen became the national champion and set a new short program record with 72.82 points.

Season Notes

2010–11

Short Program music: "On Golden Pond" by Dave Grusin
Long Program music: "My Sweet and Tender Beast" by Eugen Doga

2011–12

SP music: "The Chairman's Waltz" by John Williams
LP music: Selections from *The Godfather* soundtrack by Nino Rota

2012–13

SP music: Music from *The House of Flying Daggers* soundtrack by Shigeru Umebayashi
LP music: "Fantasy for Violin and Orchestra" by Joshua Bell

Competition dresses designed by Karen's mom, Hsiu-Hui Tseng

2013–14

SP music: "Esperanza" by Maxime Rodriguez

LP music: Selections from the *Miss Saigon* soundtrack by Claude-Michel Schönberg

2014–15

SP music: "Requiem for a Tower" by Clint Mansell

LP music: "The Godfather Suite" by Carmine Coppola and Nino Rota

Competition dresses designed by Lilya Dukler (SP) and Elena Pollack (LP).

2015–16

SP music: "Nessun Dorma" by Puccini

LP music: Selections from *Les Misérables* by Claude-Michel Schönberg

Both dresses designed by Lisa McKinnon

2016–17

SP music: "On Golden Pond" by Dave Grusin

LP music: Jalousie "Tango Tzigane" aka "Jealousy Tango" by Jacob Gade

Both dresses designed by Lisa McKinnon

2017–18

SP music: "El Tango de Roxanne" from *Moulin Rouge*, sung by José Feliciano

LP music: *Carmen Suite* after Bizet's opera, by Rodion Shchedrin

FIGURE SKATING COMPETITIVE SEASON TIMELINE

- Seasons begin in July and extend through June of the next year, and events are all sanctioned by the International Skating Union.
- ISU Grand Prix of Figure Skating events are invitationals that run from October through December.
- ISU Challenger Series events are ranked below the Grand Prix series; skaters can enter a maximum of three Challenger events.

July and August
Unofficial showcase events

September
US International Classic (Challenger)
Autumn Classic (Challenger)

October
Skate America (Grand Prix)
Skate Canada (Grand Prix)

November
Cup of China (Grand Prix)
NHK Trophy (Grand Prix)

December
Golden Spin of Zagreb (Challenger)
Grand Prix Final (Grand Prix)

January
US Figure Skating Championships
Four Continents Championships (ISU Championships)

February
Winter Olympics (every four years)

March
World Championships

April
World Team Trophy

GLOSSARY OF FIGURE SKATING TERMS

Technical Terms

ACCOUNTANT
An official at a figure skating competition who compiles and computes marks awarded by judges to determine the placement of competitors.

AXEL JUMP
One of the most difficult jumps, which takes off from the forward outside edge and is landed on the back outside edge of the opposite foot. A single axel consists of 1.5 revolutions, a double is 2.5 revolutions, and a triple is

3.5 revolutions. The jump is named for its inventor, Axel Paulsen. It is easily recognizable, as it is the only jump that takes off from a forward position.

BIELLMANN POSITION
Named after Denise Biellmann, this is a difficult variation where the skater's free leg is pulled from behind to a position higher than and toward the top of the head.

BRACKET
A turn from forward to backward or backward to forward that is executed on one foot in the direction opposite the curve from an outside edge to an inside edge or vice versa, with the exit curve continuing on the same lobe as the entry curve. The pattern the turn creates on the ice looks like a bracket ({).

CAMEL SPIN
A spin that is done on one leg, with the non-skating leg, or free leg, extended backward with knee higher than hip level. The body remains in this "spiral" position while spinning.

CHOCTAW
A turn from forward to backward (or backward to forward) from one foot to the other in which the curve of

the exit edge is in the opposite direction to the curve of the entry edge. The change of foot is from outside edge to inside edge or from inside edge to outside edge.

COMBINATION SPIN

A spin in which the skater changes feet and/or positions.

COUNTER

A turn made on one foot from a forward to backward (or backward to forward) edge maintaining the same character, i.e., outside to outside or inside to inside, where the body rotation is counter to the natural direction of progress.

CROSSOVERS

A method of gaining speed and turning corners in which skaters cross one foot over the other. There are both forward and backward crossovers.

DANCE LIFTS

A movement in which one of the partners is elevated with active and/or passive assistance of the other partner to any permitted height, sustained there and set down on the ice. Any rotations and positions and changes of positions during the lift are permitted. Lifts should enhance the music and be performed in an elegant manner.

DEATH SPIRAL

A pairs move in which the man rotates in a pivot position while holding one hand of his partner, who is rotating in a horizontal position around him with her body low and parallel to the ice.

DIFFICULT VARIATION

A movement of a body part that requires physical strength or flexibility and has an effect on the balance of the main body core. Only these variations can increase the level of an element.

DOWNGRADED

A jump, throw jump, or twist lift that is missing one-half revolution or more. A downgraded jump is indicated on a skater protocol with a "<<"symbol and receives the value for the jump of one rotation less (i.e., a downgraded triple loop will receive the value of a double loop).

DRAW

The process to determine the starting or skating order for each event. Either the referee or chair of the competition conducts the process in the presence of other judges (closed draw) or in an open setting where the athletes participate and actually draw a number from a pouch (open draw).

EDGES

The two sides of the skate blade on either side of the grooved center. There is an inside edge—the edge on the inner side of the leg—and an outside edge—the edge on the outer side of the leg. There is a forward and backward for each edge and each side, equaling a total of eight different edges.

EDGE JUMP

A jump where the skater takes off from the entry edge of the skating foot without bringing the free foot in contact with the ice to assist the takeoff. The axel, loop, and Salchow are common edge jumps.

ELIGIBLE

The term used to define skaters or competitions that meet the requirements and follow the rules of US Figure Skating and/or the International Skating Union (ISU). All eligible skaters, judges, and officials are members of US Figure Skating and have not participated in any activities, competitions, or events that are not sanctioned by US Figure Skating or the ISU.

ENVELOPE SYSTEM

In the United States, the envelope system is a part of the US National Team and separates skaters for ASUPP funding levels. Based on prescribed criteria, US athletes can be placed in Team A, B, C, the reserve team, or the developmental team. The US Figure Skating Athlete Support Fund (ASUPP) financially supports the US Team envelope athletes by assisting them with their skating expenses.

FEATURES
Additions that make elements more difficult and increase the base value.

FLIP JUMP
A toe-pick-assisted jump taken off from the back inside edge of one foot and landed on the back outside edge of the opposite foot.

FLYING SPIN
A spin in which the entrance is a jump. No rotation on the ice is permitted before the takeoff.

FOOTWORK
A series of steps and turns that immediately follow one another, executed in time to the music and choreographically related to one another. Also referred to as a step sequence, footwork is intended to show the precision and dexterity of the skater's movements.

FREE DANCE

The free dance is relatively unrestricted, and skaters select the mood and tempo as long as it is danceable. Couples (for senior level) are allowed four minutes to display their full range of technical skills, interpretation, and inventiveness. It is preceded by the short dance.

FREE SKATE (OR FREE SKATING)

The free skate does not have required elements, so skaters select their own music and theme and choreograph the many difficult jumps, spins, and step sequences that best display their technical and artistic skills. The free skate (for senior level) has a length of four and a half minutes for men and pairs, and four minutes for ladies. It is preceded by the short program.

HAND-TO-HAND LOOP LIFT

A press lift in which the man raises his partner, who is in front of him and facing the same direction, above his head. She remains facing the same direction, in the sitting position with her hands behind her, while her partner supports her by the hands.

HYDRANT LIFT

A lift in which the man throws his partner over his head while skating backward, rotates one-half turn, and catches his partner facing him.

INTERMEDIATE SPIN POSITION

Any position that does not fit the definition of a camel, sit, or upright position.

JUMP COMBINATION

A jump element consisting of two or three listed jumps where the landing foot of one jump is the takeoff foot of the next jump.

JUMP ELEMENT

An individual jump, a jump combination, or a jump sequence. Singles and pairs skaters are limited in the number of jump elements they can attempt in a program.

JUMP SEQUENCE

A jump element consisting of any number of listed jumps that are linked by nonlisted jumps and/or hops immediately following one another while maintaining the jump rhythm. There can be no turns, steps, crossovers, or stroking during the sequence.

LASSO LIFT

A hand-to-hand overhead lift in which the man swings his partner from one side of his body, around behind his head, and into a raised position. Once in the lift, the lady is in a split position facing the same direction as the man. There are four different types of lasso lifts, determined by the takeoff: toe lasso, step in lasso, reverse lasso, and axel lasso.

LAYBACK SPIN ∽

Generally performed by women, the layback spin involves an upright spin position where the head and shoulders are dropped backward and the back arches.

LEVEL OF DIFFICULTY

A measure of the complexity of an element. Skaters can achieve higher levels of difficulty through the use of features. In singles, pairs, and ice dancing, levels range from 1 to 4, with Level 1 having the lowest base value and Level 4 having the highest base value.

LISTED JUMP

A jump that is listed in the scale of values. Listed jumps are defined by their takeoff. There are six different types of listed jumps: toe loop, Salchow, loop, flip, lutz, and axel.

LIFTS

Pair moves in which the man lifts his partner above his head with arm(s) fully extended. Lifts consist of precise ascending, rotational, and descending movements.

LOBE
The pattern made on the ice by an edge or steps, forming an arc of a circle that starts and finishes on an axis.

LONG LIFTS
Dance lifts with a maximum duration of twelve seconds. There are three different types: reverse rotational, serpentine, and combination.

LONG PROGRAM
Old term for the free skate portion of the singles and pairs competitions.

LOOP
A one-foot movement where the skater skates an oval pattern within a circle without changing direction or edge. The entry and exit of the loop must cross.

LOOP JUMP
An edge jump, taken off from a back outside edge and landed on the same back outside edge.

LUTZ JUMP
A toe-pick-assisted jump taken off from a back outside

edge and landed on the back outside edge of the opposite foot. The skater glides backward on a wide curve, taps his toe pick into the ice, and rotates in the opposite direction of the curve. The jump is named for its inventor, Alois Lutz.

MIRROR SKATING

Any movements in pairs skating or ice dancing where the partners perform the same movements but in opposite directions, thus creating a mirror-image effect.

MOHAWK

A turn from forward to backward (or backward to forward), from one foot to the other, each edge forming parts of the same curve.

MOVES IN THE FIELD

One of three test structures in US Figure Skating, moves-in-the-field tests help develop all basic fundamental edges and turns while emphasizing edge quality, extension, quickness, and power.

NONLISTED JUMPS

Jumps that are not listed in the scale of values and do not count as jump elements that can be used throughout a program to enhance the choreography. Such jumps are typically one revolution or less.

NONQUALIFYING COMPETITION

Also referred to as a club competition, nonqualifying events are those that are not part of the US qualifying structure leading up to the US Championships.

ORIGINAL DANCE

The second competition phase in ice dancing that falls after the pattern dance and before the free dance. Skaters are given a prescribed rhythm (such as the paso doble or rhumba) with a defined tempo range and must create a completely original version of the dance. It has a time limit of two and a half minutes.

OVERHEAD LIFTS

The group of pair lifts in which one or both of the man's arms are fully extended as he holds his partner overhead. The man does not let go of his partner during the lift, except momentarily during changes in her position or during the dismount.

PAIRS LIFTS

Lifts done in pairs skating, which are classified into five groups. Group 1 = armpit hold position. Group 2 = waist hold position. Group 3 = hand-to-hip or upper part of the leg (above the knee) position. Group 4 = hand-to-hand press position. Group 5 = hand-to-hand lasso position.

Groups are listed in order of difficulty from easiest to most difficult; however, Groups 3 and 4 are of the same difficulty. Senior pairs teams are most likely to perform lifts from Groups 3, 4, and 5.

PATTERN DANCE

A dance that has prescribed rhythms and specific steps that must be done in an exact manner with exact placement on the ice.

PLATTER LIFT

A hand-to-hip lift in which the man raises his partner overhead with his hands resting on her hips. She is horizontal to the ice, facing the back of the man, in a platter position.

PRESS LIFT

A hand-to-hand overhead lift in which the man presses the lady into the air above his head. The partners may be face-to-face on the takeoff, or they may both be traveling backward, with the lady in front of the man.

PROTOCOL

A term used to describe the individual score sheet that each skater receives after completing a program in a competition judged using the international judging system.

This score sheet shows every element attempted in a program, how the element was called by the technical panel and scored by the judges in grade of execution (GOE), the points received for each element, and the program component scores received from the judges.

QUALIFYING COMPETITION

In the United States, qualifying competitions are those that are part of the competition structure leading to the US Championships, US Adult Championships, US Synchronized Team Skating Championships, and US Junior Championships. Qualifying competitions are all regional and sectional events.

REFEREE

The official at a competition who has full authority over all aspects of the event and is the chairperson for the panel of judges. It is the referee's responsibility to ensure that all rules are observed, that a high standard of judging is maintained, and that all technical aspects of the competition are satisfactory.

REGIONALS

The regional championships are the first step in the US qualifying competition structure that leads to the US Championships. US Figure Skating currently breaks down the United States into nine regional areas and competitions. Skaters must place in the top four at their regional event to advance to sectionals (the second step in the qualifying competition structure). Juvenile and intermediate skaters go directly from regionals to the US Junior Championships (top four places only).

ROCKER

A turn executed on one foot from a forward to backward (or backward to forward) edge maintaining the same character, i.e., inside to inside or outside to outside, where the body rotation is in the same direction as the natural progress.

SALCHOW

Another edge jump taken off from the back inside edge of one foot and landed on the back outside edge of the opposite foot. Created by Ulrich Salchow.

SANCTION

Permission or approval given by US Figure Skating or the ISU to member clubs, competition organizers, individuals, or national federations to conduct competitions, shows, or events featuring eligible athletes. Registered US Figure Skating athletes can only participate in sanctioned activities to remain eligible.

SCRATCH SPIN

Also known as an upright spin. After entering from a controlled forward outside edge, the spin begins on a back inside edge. Gradual acceleration begins by moving and placing the free foot toward the top of the skating knee and drawing the arms close to the body. The spin exits into a backward outside edge.

SECTIONALS

The sectional championships are the second and final step in the US qualifying competition structure that leads to the US Championships. The top four finishers from each sectional advance to the US Championships. There are currently three sectionals—Eastern, Mid-western, and Pacific Coast—within US Figure Skating competition structure.

SET OF SEQUENTIAL TWIZZLES

An element performed in the short dance consisting of two twizzles skated simultaneously by both partners with up to one step in between the twizzles.

SET OF SYNCHRONIZED TWIZZLES

An element performed in the free dance consisting of two twizzles performed simultaneously by both partners with up to three steps in between the twizzles.

SHADOW SKATING

Any movement in pairs skating performed by both partners simultaneously while skating in close proximity.

SHORT DANCE

The short dance consists of required elements including dance lifts, spins, twizzles, step sequences, and sequences or sections of pattern dances. Teams choose their own music and choreography, but they must conform to the specified rhythms and requirements. For 2010–2011, the specified pattern dance within the short dance (for the senior level) was the Golden Waltz. Couples can choose up to two additional rhythms from the following: foxtrot, quickstep, tango.

SHORT LIFTS

Dance lifts with a maximum duration of six seconds. There are four different types: stationary, straight line, curve, and rotational.

SHORT PROGRAM

Official name for a two-minute, fifty-second program in singles and pairs that consists of eight required elements and is set to music of the skater's choice. No more than eight required elements can be done. It is followed by the free skate.

SIT SPIN
A spin that is done in a "sitting" position with the upper part of the skating leg at least parallel to the ice.

SPIRAL
A position with one blade on the ice and the free leg (including knee and foot) higher than hip level. Spiral positions are classified according to the skating leg (right or left), edge (outside or inside), direction (forward or backward) and position of the free leg (backward, forward, or sideways).

SPIRAL SEQUENCE
A sequence of steps that incorporates various spirals in a pattern across the ice. Spirals in a spiral sequence may be done going forward, backward, in a straight line or on a curve, or on an inside or an outside edge.

STAR LIFT
A hand-to-hip lift in which the man raises his partner by her hip, from his side into the air. Her legs are in a scissor position, with either one hand touching his shoulder, or both hands free.

STARTING ORDER
The result of the draw, which lists the order in which the

athletes will compete and the group in which each athlete will warm up prior to competition.

STEP SEQUENCE

A sequence of steps and turns that immediately follow one another, executed in time to the music and choreographically related to one another.

STROKING

Fluid movement used to gain speed in which a skater pushes off back and forth from the inside edge of one skate to the inside edge of the other skate.

SWIZZLE

A method of two-foot progression, either forward or backward, by an in-and-out movement of the feet on inside edges.

TECHNICAL PROGRAM

Former term for the short program.

THREE TURN

A turn from forward to backward or backward to forward that is executed on one foot in the direction of the curve from an outside edge to an inside edge or vice versa, with the exit curve continuing on the same lobe as the entry curve. The pattern the turn creates on the ice looks like a "3."

THROW JUMP

A pairs move in which the male partner assists the woman into the air; she then executes one, two, three, or four revolutions and lands skating backward.

TOE LOOP

A toe-pick-assisted jump that takes off and lands on the same back outside edge.

TOE OVERHEAD LIFT

A lift in which the man swings his partner from one side of his body, around behind his head, and into a raised position. She is facing the same direction as the man in a split position.

TOE PICKS

The teeth at the front of the blade used primarily for jumping and spinning.

TWIST LIFTS

The group of pairs lifts where both partners begin skating backward, and the man lifts his partner over his head and tosses her in the air. While airborne, she will execute full or half rotations. The man catches his partner and places her back on the ice.

TWIZZLE

A traveling turn on one foot with one or more rotations, which is quickly rotated with a continuous (uninterrupted) action. The weight remains on the skating foot, with the free foot in any position during the turn, and then is placed beside the skating foot to skate the next steps.

UNDER-ROTATED JUMP

A jump or throw jump that is missing more than one-quarter but less than one-half revolution. Such a jump is indicated on a skater protocol with a "<" symbol and receives 70 percent of the base value of the intended jump.

UPRIGHT SPIN

Any position with the skating leg extended or almost extended that is not a camel position.

Terms Applying to the International Judging System

THE PLAYERS

TECHNICAL PANEL

Consists of five people who work as a team and have direct communication with one another in running the ISU judging system. These positions include a technical controller, a technical specialist, assistant technical specialist, data operator, and a video replay operator. All final decisions made on elements and levels will be made from the majority opinion of the first three technical positions.

TECHNICAL SPECIALIST (CALLER)

The person who identifies and calls performed elements and their level of difficulty. This person has the highest knowledge of figure skating or ice dancing.

TECHNICAL SCORE

BASE VALUE

A value assigned to each element depending on the degree of difficulty.

GRADE OF EXECUTION (GOE)

The grade of execution, ranging from -3 to +3, that is given for every element per the judge's discretion.

SCALE OF VALUES

Determines how much each performed element is worth.

PROGRAM COMPONENTS
CHOREOGRAPHY/COMPOSITION

An intentional, developed and/or original arrangement of all types of movements according to the principles of proportion, unity, space, pattern, structure, and phrasing.

INTERPRETATION

The personal and creative translation of the music to movement on ice.

PERFORMANCE/EXECUTION

Performance is the involvement of the skater/couple/ teams physically, emotionally, and intellectually as they translate the intent of the music and choreography. Execution is the quality of movement and precision in delivery. This includes harmony of movement in pairs and ice dancing.

PROGRAM COMPONENTS

The program components are the five components that express the overall presentation: skating skills, transitions, performance/execution, choreography/com-position, and interpretation. The compulsory dance(s) in ice dancing uses one additional component: timing.

SKATING SKILLS

Overall skating quality: edge control and flow over the ice surface demonstrated by a command of the skating vocabulary (edges, steps, turns, etc.), the clarity of technique, and use of effortless power to accelerate and vary speed.

TRANSITIONS/LINKING FOOTWORK AND MOVEMENTS

The varied and/or intricate footwork, positions, movements, and holds that link all elements. In singles, pairs, and synchronized, this also includes the entrances and exits of technical elements.

SCORING

COMPETITION SCORE (FINAL SCORE)

The qualifying segment score (x 0.25) + short program segment score + free skate segment score, or the compulsory dance segment score + original dance segment score + free dance segment score.

INTERNATIONAL SKATING UNION TECHNICAL RULES

Rule 500: Definition of the Skate Blade

Figure skating blades used during competitions must be sharpened to produce a flat to concave cross section without change to the width of the blade as measured between the two edges. However, a slight tapering or narrowing of the cross section of the blade is permitted.

Rule 501: Clothing

At ISU Championships, the Olympic Winter Games, and international competitions, the clothing of the competitors must be modest, dignified, and appropriate for athletic competition—not garish or theatrical in design. Clothing may, however, reflect the character of the music chosen. The clothing must not give the effect of excessive nudity inappropriate for the discipline. Men must wear full-length trousers and must not wear tights. In addition, in ice dance, ladies must wear a skirt. Accessories and props are not permitted.

Skating Skills

Defined by overall cleanness and sureness, edge control and flow over the ice surface demonstrated by a command of the skating vocabulary (edges, steps, turns, etc.), the clarity of technique, and the use of effortless power to accelerate and vary speed.

In evaluating the skating skills, the following must be considered:

- Use of deep edges, steps, and turns;
- Balance, rhythmic knee action, and precision of foot placement;
- Flow and glide;
- Varied use of power, speed, and acceleration;
- Use of multidirectional skating;
- Use of one-foot skating.

Transitions

The varied and purposeful use of intricate footwork, positions, movements, and holds that link all elements.

In evaluating the transitions, the following must be considered:

- Continuity of movements from one element to another (all disciplines);
- Variety;
- Difficulty;
- Quality.

Performance

Involvement of the skater/pair/couple physically, emotionally, and intellectually as they deliver the intent of the music and composition.

In evaluating the performance, the following must be considered:

- Physical, emotional, intellectual involvement and projection;
- Carriage and clarity of movement;
- Variety and contrast of movements and energy;
- Individuality/personality.

Composition

An intentionally developed and/or original arrangement of all types of movements according to the principles of musical phrase, space, pattern, and structure.

In evaluating the composition, the following must be considered:

- Purpose (idea, concept, vision, mood);
- Pattern/ice coverage;
- Multidimensional use of space and design of movements;
- Phrase and form (movements and parts structured to match the musical phrase);
- Originality of the composition.

US FIGURE SKATING CHAMPIONSHIPS—SINGLE LADIES CHAMPIONS

Year	Location	Gold	Silver	Bronze	Pewter
1914	New Haven	Theresa Weld	Edith Rotch	Raynham Townshend	
1918	New York City	Rosemary Beresford	Theresa Weld		
1920	New York City	Theresa Weld	Martha Brown	Lilian Cramer	
1921	Philadelphia	Theresa Weld Blanchard	Lilian Cramer		
1922	Boston	Theresa Weld Blanchard	Beatrix Loughran		
1923	New Haven	Theresa Weld Blanchard	Beatrix Loughran	Lilian Cramer	
1924	Philadelphia	Theresa Weld Blanchard	Rosalie Knapp		
1925	New York City	Beatrix Loughran	Theresa Weld Blanchard	Rosalie Knapp	
1926	Boston	Beatrix Loughran	Theresa Weld Blanchard	Maribel Vinson	

Year	Location	Gold	Silver	Bronze	Pewter
1927	New York City	Beatrix Loughran	Maribel Vinson	Theresa Weld Blanchard	
1928	New Haven	Maribel Vinson	Suzanne Davis		
1929	New York City	Maribel Vinson	Edith Secord	Suzanne Davis	
1930	Providence	Maribel Vinson	Edith Secord	Suzanne Davis	
1931	Boston	Maribel Vinson	Edith Secord	Hulda Berger	
1932	New York City	Maribel Vinson	Margaret Bennett	Louise Weigel	
1933	New Haven	Maribel Vinson	Suzanne Davis	Louise Weigel	
1934	Philadelphia	Suzanne Davis	Louise Weigel	Estelle Weigel	
1935	New Haven	Maribel Vinson	Suzanne Davis	Louise Weigel	
1936	New York City	Maribel Vinson	Louise Weigel	Audrey Peppe	
1937	Chicago	Maribel Vinson	Polly Blodgett	Katherine Durbrow	
1938	Philadelphia	Joan Tozzer	Audrey Peppe	Polly Blodgett	Jane Vaughn
1939	St. Paul	Joan Tozzer	Audrey Peppe	Charlotte Walther	
1940	Cleveland	Joan Tozzer	Hedy Stenuf	Jane Vaughn	
1941	Boston	Jane Vaughn	Gretchen Merrill	Charlotte Walther	
1942	Chicago	Jane Vaughn Sullivan	Gretchen Merrill	Phebe Tucker	
1943	New York City	Gretchen Merrill	Dorothy Goos	Janette Ahrens	
1944	Minneapolis	Gretchen Merrill	Dorothy Goos	Ramona Allen	
1945	New York City	Gretchen Merrill	Janette Ahrens	Madelon Olson	
1946	Chicago	Gretchen Merrill	Janette Ahrens	Madelon Olson	
1947	Berkeley	Gretchen Merrill	Janette Ahrens	Eileen Seigh	
1948	Colorado Springs	Gretchen Merrill	Yvonne C. Sherman	Helen Uhl	

Year	Location	Gold	Silver	Bronze	Pewter
1949	Colorado Springs	Yvonne C. Sherman	Gretchen Merrill	Virginia Baxter	
1950	Washington, DC	Yvonne C. Sherman	Sonya Klopfer	Virginia Baxter	
1951	Seattle	Sonya Klopfer	Tenley Albright	Virginia Baxter	
1952	Colorado Springs	Tenley Albright	Frances Dorsey	Helen Geekie	
1953	Hershey	Tenley Albright	Carol Heiss	Margaret Graham	Margaret Dean
1954	Los Angeles	Tenley Albright	Carol Heiss	Frances Dorsey	Margaret Graham
1955	Colorado Springs	Tenley Albright	Carol Heiss	Catherine Machado	Patricia Firth
1956	Philadelphia	Tenley Albright	Carol Heiss	Catherine Machado	Mary Anne Dorsey
1957	Berkeley	Carol Heiss	Joan Schenke	Claralynn Lewis	Nancy Heiss
1958	Minneapolis	Carol Heiss	Carol Wanek	Lynn Finnegan	Nancy Heiss
1959	Rochester	Carol Heiss	Nancy Heiss	Barbara Roles	Lynn Finnegan
1960	Seattle	Carol Heiss	Barbara Roles	Laurence Owen	Stephanie Westerfield
1961	Colorado Springs	Laurence Owen	Stephanie Westerfield	Rhode Lee Michelson	Karen Howland
1962	Boston	Barbara Roles Pursley	Lorraine Hanlon	Victoria Fisher	Frances Gold
1963	Long Beach	Lorraine Hanlon	Christine Haigler	Karen Howland	
1964	Cleveland	Peggy Fleming	Albertina Noyes	Christine Haigler	Lorraine Hanlon
1965	Lake Placid	Peggy Fleming	Christine Haigler	Albertina Noyes	Myrna Bodek
1966	Berkeley	Peggy Fleming	Albertina Noyes	Pamela Schneider	
1967	Omaha	Peggy Fleming	Albertina Noyes	Jennie Walsh	Janet Lynn
1968	Philadelphia	Peggy Fleming	Albertina Noyes	Janet Lynn	
1969	Seattle	Janet Lynn	Julie Lynn Holmes	Albertina Noyes	Dawn Glab
1970	Tulsa	Janet Lynn	Julie Lynn Holmes	Dawn Glab	Jennie Walsh

Year	Location	Gold	Silver	Bronze	Pewter
1971	Buffalo	Janet Lynn	Julie Lynn Holmes	Suna Murray	Dawn Glab
1972	Long Beach	Janet Lynn	Julie Lynn Holmes	Suna Murray	Dorothy Hamill
1973	Minneapolis	Janet Lynn	Dorothy Hamill	Juli McKinstry	
1974	Providence	Dorothy Hamill	Juli McKinstry	Kath Malmberg	
1975	Oakland	Dorothy Hamill	Wendy Burge	Kath Malmberg	Barbie Smith
1976	Colorado Springs	Dorothy Hamill	Linda Fratianne	Wendy Burge	Kath Malmberg
1977	Hartford	Linda Fratianne	Barbie Smith	Wendy Burge	
1978	Portland	Linda Fratianne	Lisa-Marie Allen	Priscilla Hill	Carrie Rugh
1979	Cincinnati	Linda Fratianne	Lisa-Marie Allen	Carrie Rugh	Alicia Risberg
1980	Atlanta	Linda Fratianne	Lisa-Marie Allen	Sandy Lenz	Elaine Zayak
1981	San Diego	Elaine Zayak	Priscilla Hill	Lisa-Marie Allen	Rosalynn Sumners
1982	Indianapolis	Rosalynn Sumners	Vikki de Vries	Elaine Zayak	Jackie Farrell
1983	Pittsburgh	Rosalynn Sumners	Elaine Zayak	Tiffany Chin	Vikki de Vries
1984	Salt Lake City	Rosalyn Sumners	Tiffany Chin	Elaine Zayak	Jill Frost
1985	Kansas City	Tiffany Chin	Debi Thomas	Caryn Kadavy	Kathryn Adams
1986	Uniondale	Debi Thomas	Caryn Kadavy	Tiffany Chin	Tracey Damigella
1987	Tacoma	Jill Trenary	Debi Thomas	Caryn Kadavy	Tiffany Chin
1988	Denver	Debi Thomas	Jill Trenary	Caryn Kadavy	Jeri Campbell
1989	Baltimore	Jill Trenary	Kristi Yamaguchi	Tonya Harding	Holly Cook
1990	Salt Lake City	Jill Trenary	Kristi Yamaguchi	Holly Cook	Nancy Kerrigan
1991	Minneapolis	Tonya Harding	Kristi Yamaguchi	Nancy Kerrigan	Tonia Kwiatkowski
1992	Orlando	Kristi Yamaguchi	Nancy Kerrigan	Tonya Harding	Lisa Ervin

Year	Location	Gold	Silver	Bronze	Pewter
1993	Phoenix	Nancy Kerrigan	Lisa Ervin	Tonia Kwiatkowski	Tonya Harding
1994	Detroit		Michelle Kwan	Nicole Bobek	Elaine Zayak
1995	Providence	Nicole Bobek	Michelle Kwan	Tonia Kwiatkowski	Kyoko Ina
1996	San Jose	Michelle Kwan	Tonia Kwiatkowski	Tara Lapinksi	Sydne Vogel
1997	Nashville	Tara Lipinski	Michelle Kwan	Nicole Bobek	Angela Nikodinov
1998	Philadelphia	Michelle Kwan	Tara Lipinski	Nicole Bobek	Tonia Kwiatkowski
1999	Salt Lake City	Michelle Kwan	Naomi Nari Nam	Angela Nikodinov	Sarah Hughes
2000	Cleveland	Michelle Kwan	Sasha Cohen	Sarah Hughes	Angela Nikodinov
2001	Boston	Michelle Kwan	Sarah Hughes	Angela Nikodinov	Jennifer Kirk
2002	Los Angeles	Michelle Kwan	Sasha Cohen	Sarah Hughes	Angela Nikodinov
2003	Dallas	Michelle Kwan	Sarah Hughes	Sasha Cohen	Ann Patrice McDonough
2004	Atlanta	Michelle Kwan	Sasha Cohen	Jennifer Kirk	Amber Corwin
2005	Portland	Michelle Kwan	Sasha Cohen	Kimmie Meissner	Jennifer Kirk
2006	St. Louis	Sasha Cohen	Kimmie Meissner	Emily Hughes	Katy Taylor
2007	Spokane	Kimmie Meissner	Emily Hughes	Alissa Czisny	Beatrisa Liang
2008	St. Paul	Mirai Nagasu	Rachael Flatt	Ashley Wagner	Caroline Zhang
2009	Cleveland	Alissa Czisny	Rachael Flatt	Caroline Zhang	Ashley Wagner
2010	Spokane	Rachael Flatt	Mirai Nagasu	Ashley Wagner	Sasha Cohen
2011	Greensboro	Alissa Czisny	Rachael Flatt	Mirai Nagasu	Agnes Zawadzki
2012	San Jose	Ashley Wagner	Alissa Czisny	Agnes Zawadzki	Caroline Zhang
2013	Omaha	Ashley Wagner	Gracie Gold	Agnes Zawadzki	Courtney Hicks
2014	Boston	Gracie Gold	Polina Edmunds	Mirai Nagasu	Ashley Wagner

KAREN CHEN

Year	Location	Gold	Silver	Bronze	Pewter
2015	Greensboro	Ashley Wagner	Gracie Gold	Karen Chen	Polina Edmunds
2016	Saint Paul	Gracie Gold	Polina Edmunds	Ashley Wagner	Mirai Nagasu
2017	Kansas City	Karen Chen	Ashley Wagner	Mariah Bell	Mirai Nagasu
2018	San Jose				

ACKNOWLEDGMENTS

HONESTLY, THERE ARE JUST SO MANY PEOPLE THAT I have met and come across in my life who have helped me so much. I may not be able to thank everyone individually in the next few pages, but if you have cheered for me in any way along my ongoing journey, I just wanted to say thank you so much for your continued support. I really, truly appreciate it from the bottom of my heart.

However, if there's anyone I need to thank first, it would be my entire family. They have been there for me when I needed them most no matter where I am and what I am doing. My parents especially; my mom, Hsiu-Hui, and my dad, Ken, have showered me with unconditional support and love that I will be eternally grateful for. I wouldn't be here if it wasn't for their sacrifices; I wouldn't be here if it wasn't for their hard work and endless efforts to help support me in every unthinkable and unimaginable way. I also can't express how much my brother has impacted my life as well. Sure we may bicker over little things, but he knows how much he means to me and I don't know where I'd be if he had never entered my life. Also, I need to thank my aunt, Trinity, and my uncle, Steven, and of course their son, Tristan, for always cheering me up and making me laugh. Lastly, I want to send a special thank-you to my grandparents, who mean the world to me. I truly can't express how thankful I am for my family. My entire family, even the ones I don't see often in Taiwan, all play a significant role in my life. They all inspire me so much in a variety of ways.

I am also extremely grateful to have met Kristi Yamaguchi and to have her support in my journey. She's everything I aspire to be, and I can't thank her enough for everything. I am incredibly honored to be able to talk to her and have her as my mentor; and especially for agreeing to write the foreword for this book!

I would like to send a bunch of thank-yous to my coaches as well. Thank you, Crystal, for helping me discover what skating is and feels like. Thank you, Sherri, for teaching me a little bit of everything. Thank you, Gilley, for always believing in me even when I didn't believe in myself; the amount of life lessons I learned from you are countless. And thank you so much Tammy for pushing me, helping me, and believing in me especially during these recent years. I have grown so much and will hopefully continue to do so on the ice with your guidance.

Lots of hugs to all the people who I have crossed paths with at the rink in Fremont, Riverside, and plenty of other rinks! The rink is part of me and the people who I've met at the rink I will never forget. You all have made training fun and enjoyable even though there were definitely some dramatic rough times for all of us. I'm sorry I can't individually thank each and every one of you (there are too many of you!), but the bottom line is, we all share the same interest on the ice and it's what I've learned to really appreciate, so thank you so much!

There is a very special childhood friend I would like to thank individually. Claire, thank you so much for accepting my craziness and for still keeping in touch with me through all these years. Thank you especially for staying up late at night and practically getting no sleep on a weekday to cheer for me and watch me skate live at worlds in Helsinki. You're the best!

Also, I wanted to give a quick but extremely sincere and generous thank-you to everyone at US Figure Skating for helping me to achieve the goals I set for myself.

Thank you for giving me such amazing opportunities in my unpredictable skating journey.

A big hug to my agent, Yuki Sageusa at IMG, for convincing me to take this wonderful opportunity of putting my skating journey into words! I am so fortunate to have you help me manage everything and for all the effort you put in. Thank you also to Lynn Plage for handling my publicity on and off the ice.

I am also extremely thankful to have such an amazing team at HarperCollins Children's Books to help me with this book project. Thank you, Natalie England, for putting in so much time and effort in writing this book. A very special thank-you to Sara Sargent, who gave me this opportunity and contributed so much to this book. Thank you, Jenna Stempel, for putting together such a beautiful design that we all love immensely. Thank you, Meaghan Finnerty, Cindy Hamilton, and Mitch Thorpe for playing such an important role in this whole exciting process! Lastly, thank you to Jamie Carr at WME for all of your help and coordination of this book.

And last, but not least, a beautifully huge thank-you to all those who supported me and took the time to read this book! I really, truly appreciate it from the bottom of my heart!

xoxo